CH

BORN in 1899, Frederick Coutts became a Salvation Army officer from Batley in 1920, serving initially in divisional and corps appointments. He then spent 18 years fulfilling roles in the Literary Department, including two years as Literary Secretary, before becoming Principal of the International Training College (now William Booth College) from 1953-57.

He was Territorial Commander in the Australian Eastern Territory until 1963 when he was elected as The Salvation Army's international leader, serving in that capacity until retirement in 1969. Having written more than a dozen books during his active officership, General Coutts continued his authorship in retirement, until his promotion to Glory in 1986.

ESSENTIALS
OF CHRISTIAN
EXPERIENCE

by

Frederick Coutts

Salvation Books
The Salvation Army International Headquarters
London, United Kingdom

First published in 1969
Second edition 1969
ISBN 85412-058-0
Third edition 1980
ISBN 0-85412-369-5

This edition 2011

ISBN 978-0-85412-838-9

Project Editor Paul Mortlock
Cover design by Nathan Sigauke

Unless indicated otherwise, all Scripture references
are from the *King James Version* of the Bible

SALVATION BOOKS

Published by Salvation Books
The Salvation Army International Headquarters
101 Queen Victoria Street, London EC4V 4EH
United Kingdom

Printed in the UK by Page Bros., Norwich

CONTENTS

SERIES INTRODUCTION
'CLASSIC SALVATIONIST TEXTS'

THE Bible often underscores the importance of speaking into the next generation. It is for this reason that Salvation Army 'classics' are being republished. A new generation of readers needs to and wants to hear from our godly Salvationists from the past who lived out their faith and wrote about it with conviction and humility. What a heritage we have and these writings share something of the richness of it!

The psalmist David declares, 'One generation will commend your works to another; they will tell of your mighty acts. They will speak of the glorious splendour of your majesty' (Psalm 145:4-5 *NIV*). In the verses that follow he continues to explain what those of one generation will say to the next when they pass on the faith.

May the Lord draw us even closer to him as we hear with our hearts what he has spoken through his Salvationist servants. And may we be challenged not only to learn from them but also to leave a legacy ourselves in our time, through our living and our communication of the deep things of God.

General Linda Bond

Frederick Coutts
A Selected Bibliography

Half-hours with Heroes *1944*

The Timeless Prophets *1944*

Short Measure: Portrait of a Young Man
(Ernest Coutts) *1945*

The Battle and the Breeze *1946*

The First Salvationist and Other Stories *1948*

He Had No Revolver and Other Stories *1951*

The Kingdom of God *1951*

Well Played! (Albert Moss) *1953*

Portrait of a Salvationist
(Sidney Carvosso Gauntlett) *1955*

The Call to Holiness *1957*

The Armoury Commentary: the Four Gospels *1973*

The Better Fight - Volume VI of
The History of The Salvation Army 1914-1946 *1973*

The Armoury Commentary:
the New Testament Epistles *1975*

No Discharge in This War *1975*

No Continuing City *1976*

Bread for my Neighbour *1978*

In Good Company *1980*

More than one Homeland:
a Biography of Commissioner Gladys Caliss *1981*

The Splendour of Holiness *1983*

The Weapons of Goodwill - Volume VII of
The History of The Salvation Army 1946-1977 *1986*

One

The Saviour we Need

*1 John 4:14: 'The Father sent the Son to be
the Saviour of the world.'*

IT has been well said that next to the foolishness
of denying the existence of God is that of trying
to prove his existence. The Bible does neither –
but is content to affirm that he is and to declare
what he has done. In the dozen words of this
biblical sentence are set out the basic facts of the
Christian faith.

We begin with 'the Father'.

All serious thinking about life begins with the
fact that God is. The 'death of God' school is itself
dying. It remains true – as Francis Bacon said – that
'a little philosophy inclineth a man's mind to
atheism, but depth in philosophy bringeth men's
minds about to religion.' It is far too readily and
gratuitously assumed that believers in God
constitute a dwindling minority, principally drawn
from the less intelligent sections of the community.
With some the wish is father to the thought. There
are those who would like it to be that way. The fact
is, however, that there are millions of men and

women – Roman Catholics, Jews, Muslims, Orthodox, Protestant – whose first article of faith is 'I believe in God.' Not all have the same understanding of God, but all believe according to the measure of their understanding.

In February 1967 I was in Bandung, a city in Indonesia, then of over a million people [2.3 million as of 2010] and, at a weeknight meeting in a public hall, was welcomed by the Muslim representative of the Provincial Governor, himself a Muslim. The speaker referred to the Pantjasila, or five principles, upon which community life in Indonesia is based, the first of which is belief in God. To my surprise – though a welcome surprise – the congregation began to applaud. Half a dozen nuns seated in the second row applauded. Two young Dutch priests at the opposite end of the row joined in. Salvationists began to clap. Muslims shared in the sound. Soon the whole meeting was applauding. 'When I go home,' I said in response, 'I shall tell my western friends that, for the first time in my life, I have heard a public meeting applaud a declaration of belief in God.'

I know that the word 'God' did not mean the same to everyone in the hall that night but, from the initial agreement that he is, we can go on to the Christian assertion that he is the God and Father of our Lord Jesus Christ. In short, he is our Father. And if our Father, then he is the One to whom I can commit my life in trustful obedience, knowing that the Creator of all things visible and invisible is also the Father who cares for each of his children. And this faith, far from being childish or infantile, an attitude to life unworthy of a grown man, is an expression of spiritual and intellectual maturity.

On that journey I left for Indonesia from Heathrow and, as an airhostess showed me through the departure lounge, I remarked to her that the place seemed unusually quiet.

'It's been like this all day,' she answered. 'Not much American traffic either.' Inwardly I thought it an ill wind that blew no one any good. This might mean that the seat next to mine would be empty and I would have room to stretch my legs on the long journey overnight. 'Yes,' went on the hostess; 'lots of folk don't like travelling on Friday the 13th.'

Possibly some of those who don't like travelling on Friday the 13th also regard the Christian faith as intellectually unworthy of their acceptance. How mixed up can we get? There on the apron stood the Boeing, a feat of precision engineering, its four Pratt and Whitney engines each developing a thrust of 18,000 lb but, for some quirk, not to be trusted on Friday the 13th. And as I walked down the aisle looking for my seat I saw rows 10, 11, 12, 14, 15 – but not 13. The truth is that when faith goes out by the door, superstition comes in at the window. To deny God is not an act of liberation, a glorious freedom nobly gained. It is to deliver oneself over to the grosser forms of credulity, with the clear

3

possibility of descending to the level of the bushman clutching his juju.

The believer affirms that this is God's world. At the heart of things is not a dark, empty hole, but a Father to whose love we may at all times commit ourselves.

But, in the second place, it may be urged that life offers no proof of this. On the contrary, there is much in our world that challenges – if not denies – the thought that a loving God rules over the destinies of men.

For answer, take in a little more of the sentence: 'The Father sent the Son…' For it is in Jesus that we see what God is like. As a small child once said, 'Jesus came to put a face on God.' As Jesus himself said, 'He that hath seen me hath seen the Father' (John 14:9). In the words and deeds of the historic Jesus of Nazareth we see the eternal God at work in the midst of men. As John wrote at the opening to his Gospel: 'Him whom no man hath seen at any time the only begotten Son made known.'

Some account of what Jesus said and did is on record for us all to read. In the New Testament there is not one, but four selections of incidents from his life. The earliest of them, called the Gospel of Mark, first appeared soon after the great fire of Rome when Nero was Caesar; that is, some 35 years after the events therein described.

Attacks on the historicity of the Gospels can be greatly overrated. I need make no claim to divine inspiration to remember what happened 35 years ago in my life. I can remember the corps at which I was stationed; the address of the quarters; the names of the census board; many of the names on the roll. I can testify without hesitation to the name of the divisional and territorial commanders and the General of that day, and can recall in some detail events both at home and in the corps. Furthermore, there are those who can challenge or confirm my recollections of those days. How much more then…? I will not labour the obvious.

So when we read the Gospels we are doing two things. First of all, we are looking at scenes from the life of one who went about doing good. And further, in those scenes we are watching God at work, sharing the sorrows of men and, as far as men would allow him, meeting both their physical and spiritual needs.

Of course, there were men in the first century who refused God's help just as there are those who do the same in the 21st. To refuse God's help on the ground that he does not exist and then to blame him for the jam in which we find ourselves is hardly logical. But perhaps we cannot be expected to be logical when we are in trouble. Yet those who turn to him will find that even in the valley of the shadow they need fear no evil for he is with them. What he offers is something better than an explanation of the changes and chances of life – for this might still prove unsatisfying. He offers his own companionship

– as Lincoln found during the American Civil War, for a soiled depression in the margin of his Bible, still preserved in the national archives, indicates the verse to which he turned again and again: 'I sought the Lord, and he heard me, and delivered me from all my fears.'

Now finish the sentence – '...to be the Saviour of the world.'

This is what men need – a Saviour. Evidence of this is not far to seek. There is the direct evidence provided by Scripture. And there is the indirect evidence, discoverable in the world around us, of the trouble that overwhelms a man when he turns his back on his Father and Saviour. One is almost persuaded at times that some of our contemporary novels might have been written to show how sore is man's predicament when he deserts the path of righteousness. I know they are not written for that purpose, which makes their unwitting testimony all the more powerful.

Take one that made quite a furore – *Lolita*. At the beginning of the story the girl is a normal, happy person. The story ends while she is still a teenager, but with ruined looks and rope-veined hands, unmarried but soon to be a mother, refusing to live with her seducer who himself is awaiting trial on a charge of murder. I do not know what Nabokov intended to say, but I do know what his story is saying – that the way of the transgressor is hard.

Men need a Saviour to save them from

themselves. That is why the Father sent the Son into the world. And just as there is ample evidence of man's need of a Saviour, so there is ample evidence that Jesus is the Saviour they need. Again I will not quote from Scripture, though I am neither afraid nor ashamed to do so. But as some would regard such as special pleading, let it be from a paperback with which was associated the Oscar prize winning film *The Bridge on the River Kwai*.

The author, Pierre Boulle, himself a prisoner of war, describes camp conditions on successive Christmases. Christmas, 1942, saw men robbing the sick, ill treating one another, caring not whether their cobbers lived or died. Compassion had vanished. Morale was at its lowest. Despair prevailed. But on Christmas Day, 1943, 2,000 men assembled for worship, sang carols and listened to the word of God. Said one prisoner of war: 'This is a merry Christmas, especially when you compare it with last year.'

How had the change come about? Simply because two or three men had held to their faith. Their acts of self-sacrifice had silently rebuked those of the 'Hang you, Jack, I'm in the boat' school. As the author comments: 'The camp had been dominated by sickness and despair. Yet I had seen a power at work to renew many of us. Men were still men, and I had seen selfishness. But I had seen love… to see Jesus was to see in him that love which is the highest form of life.' It was Christ who made the difference to that camp. No wonder the author called his book *Miracle on the River Kwai*.

This same miracle can be repeated in the lives of all who commit themselves to Jesus as Saviour and Lord. 'The Father sent the Son to be the Saviour of the world' – and he is the Saviour we need.

Two

Image and Reality

Luke 6:46: 'Why call ye me, Lord, Lord, and do not the things which I say?'

WHEN in 1885 the Founder welcomed 'very gratefully' (to use his own words) the *English Revised Version* of the Bible, he added that he wanted 'to see a new translation of the Bible into the hearts and conduct of living men and women… This seems to me to be the only translation which will in the long run prove to be of any value. It is the reproduction of the Scriptures in men and women that makes their worth… Christian scholars have translated the Bible and retranslated it, and then translated it again… There seems to me only one thing left to be done and that is to give us a literal and faithful and understandable translation of it in practice.'

No comment could be closer in spirit to this saying of Jesus: 'Why call ye me, Lord, Lord, and do not the things which I say?'

To call Jesus Lord was to ascribe to him supreme authority. The secular significance of this title is made plain in the court scene where Paul appealed to Caesar. The charge against this unusual prisoner had the Roman procurator baffled. It fell under no legal category known to him. 'I have no certain thing to write unto my lord,' said Festus to Agrippa. The *New English Bible* translates: 'I have nothing definite about him to put in writing for our Sovereign' (Acts 25:26).

Caesar, sovereign, lord – these were titles for the supreme authority in the Roman world. And 'Lord' was the title that believers applied to Jesus. 'God hath made that same Jesus, whom ye crucified, both Lord and Christ' (Acts 2:36). If his is the name high over all, then better to never acknowledge him as such than so to address him and then disobey him. This is to fall into the greater condemnation.

Our Lord himself said this too often and too plainly for anyone to mistake his meaning. The contrasts he continually drew were between saying and doing. 'Not every one that saith unto me, Lord, Lord, shall enter into the kingdom of Heaven; but he that doeth the will of my Father which is in Heaven. Many will say to me in that day, Lord, Lord... And then will I profess unto them, I never knew you' (Matthew 7:21-23). 'Ye call me Master and Lord: and ye say well' (John 13:13). 'I have given you an example, that ye should do as I have done to you' (John 13:15). Profession without practice was worse than useless.

Men who are far from Christ agree with him on this point. It is our critics who are among the loudest in their demand that in our lives deed and word should agree. They are the first with their condemnation if, in their opinion, some believer falls below this standard. That is why the misdeed of some solitary Salvationist, overtaken in a fault, hits the headlines. It may be hard to take when those who make no profession at all sit as self constituted judges upon someone whose practice falls short of his high profession. But in his own twisted way the worldling is unwittingly agreeing with the Christian standard that 'by their fruits ye shall know them' (Matthew 7:20).

After Lenin died his widow, Nadezhda Krupskaya, was asked how best his life and work could be remembered. 'Do not let your sorrow find expression in any outward veneration of his personality,' she answered. 'Do not raise monuments to him or a palace to his name. Do not organise pompous ceremonies in his memory. In life he took little account of that kind of thing. If you want to honour his name, realise his teachings in your life.' This is what Jesus said about his teaching.

Now relate this truth to the image and experience of the Salvationist.

Much is said about the importance of the image of the Army. It is not an unworthy desire that our image should do justice to our cause. But we also know that it is beyond our skill to build up any image for public consumption that presents us in a better light than we really are. Sophisticated though a few of us may think ourselves, we are by and large too honest and simple hearted to maintain any such pose for long, even if we tried. Somebody would be sure to give it away! Besides, to attempt to project any such fictional account of ourselves would lead to the sorriest hypocrisy.

It will be known that the word hypocrite, in its earliest usage, meant 'one who answers'. Then it came to describe one who answers in a dialogue or a set piece – that is, on a stage. Afterwards it came to stand for one whose whole life was a piece of acting – just one long make-believe. We don't want ever to start on that slippery slide. And when we weigh image and reality in the inexorable scales of life itself there is no doubt which way the balance tilts.

By way of illustration, go back to a time when, in terms of current public relations, the Army's image was deplorable. To borrow a phrase used by the apostle Paul about himself, we were regarded by many as 'the scum of the earth' (1 Corinthians 4:13 *NEB*). At that period in our history the Maréchale, eldest of the Founder's four daughters, commenced our work in the city of Nîmes in the south of France. She had to face the hostility of saints and sinners alike. When one of her first meetings was opened in Army fashion for public testimony, several pastors availed themselves of this opportunity to attack the Army – particularly concerning the doctrine of holiness. Their critical remarks drew wide applause and from the congregation a voice shouted in support: 'Let him that is without sin rise and testify' (see John 8:7).

'Rise and testify, Bisson,' said the Maréchale to a recent convert who was sitting near to her. And Bisson rose to witness in his own untutored way to the divine power which both saves and keeps. The witness of his life could not be denied – as the presence of the lame man, now healed, with the apostles silenced the Sanhedrin. The glory of the reality triumphed over the poor image.

And today the value of what we profess rises or falls by the life of the anonymous soldier who lives in the London SW19 post code area, the Salvationist serviceman at Kneller Hall, the bandsman-student at a redbrick university, the member of our Nurses' Fellowship in a city hospital, the converted shop steward on the factory floor, the wife and mother on the housing estate. One godly life counts for more than a string of poster hoardings. This must not be construed as a left-handed argument against the use of current mass media. We would do the work of the Kingdom disservice to neglect these means. But do not let any Salvationist think that it no longer matters how he carries himself because in our public relations we've never had it so good. Our image will not long remain in better standing than we are ourselves. God would not be dealing faithfully with us if he allowed such a thing to happen. Take care of the reality and the image will take care of itself. We must first – and last – do the things which he says.

Now relate this command to the experience of the Salvationist as well. For what is the life of holiness but the endeavour, as God shall give us grace, to translate the gospel we preach into a pattern of daily living?

To many of our friends and neighbours the word 'gospel' – that for us covers the whole of God's wise design for man's salvation – is but a technical religious term that they no more understand than I do the technical terms employed in electronics. But by doing the things God says the gospel takes on a clear and visible outline.

When the pilgrims in Bunyan's story reached Vanity Fair they were quickly recognised for what they were by what they wore, by what they said, and by their indifference to what the shops in the city had to sell. That is to say, theirs was a distinctive pattern of living that was the outward and noticeable expression of their faith. The truth which inwardly they cherished was manifest in their conduct. So we can help to make the message clear and plain by doing what he says. John Baillie had a famous aside that being a Christian made a difference to the way a man tied up his shoes. That was his way of saying that the spirit of Jesus in a man's life is like a drop of dye in a vat of water. Test it by the bucketful or the spoonful – the colour will be of the same intensity throughout. And holiness is just such a consistent pattern of living that cannot be denied. From scheme and creed the light may go out but:

> *The blessed gospel none can doubt*
> *Revealed in holy lives.*

Most importantly of all, this word of Jesus applies to our relationship with him. For the more openly we call him Lord, the greater is our obligation to obey him, and the heavier will be our condemnation if we do not the things he says. This was the point of the parable, found in Matthew chapter 21, of the two sons who were bidden work in the vineyard. 'I go not,' said one, but afterwards repented and went. 'I go,' said the other, but went not. Which of them did the will of his father?

It is related that during the last century a missionary told this parable word for word to a Near East audience and then asked the same question.

'The second,' was the answer – he who said: 'I go,' even though he went not. And when the reason was sought for this answer, the response was that no son should say no to his father's face. That was a more grievous sin than promising and failing to keep the promise. A show of manners was deemed to be of greater worth than genuine obedience.

It is sadly true that there are some believers who are content with a show of good religious manners. They make it their business to attend the church of their choice. Their social appearance is never any discredit to their faith. They may even support the work of God in a conventional way. But when their Lord says: 'Go work,' they politely reply: 'I go,' but their word remains unsupported by action.

The question before us is: am I doing the things he says? The word that comes to us is: whatsoever he saith unto you, do it.

Three

The Work of the Spirit

Hebrews 12:14: 'Follow… holiness,
without which no man shall see the Lord.'

MANY names are given to the doctrine after which
our Sunday morning meeting for worship has long
been named. But the second blessing, Christian
perfection, entire sanctification, the blessing of
perfect love, all stand for one and the same
experience. They are varying descriptions of the
same reality, though for present purposes we will
keep to the words 'holiness' and 'holy'.

Both go back to the earliest days of the religious
education of the people of God and applied, to
begin with, to that which provoked awe.

A place could be holy. 'Put off thy shoes from
off thy feet, for the place whereon thou standest is
holy ground' (Exodus 3:5) was the word that
came to Moses. Take care; show reverence; this
ground is holy.

When the children of Israel came to Sinai,
bounds were set about the smoking mountain lest
they should unwittingly trespass on that which was
holy. Keep away; keep off, these slopes are holy.

Similarly, none but certain persons could handle the Ark for that too was holy in that it belonged to God. One man who transgressed this rule, even with the best of intentions, fell dead. Men should beware of the holy. Increasing holiness was denoted by increasing remoteness from the common man.

This idea found expression in the construction of the Jerusalem temples, the third of which was the one known to Jesus himself. Larger in construction than any of our English cathedrals, it can best be compared to a giant series of unroofed boxes, the one inside the other and all – save the last – open to the sky.

To the outer court of the Gentiles anyone might come – men, women, Jews, Gentiles, visitors, traders. This was where the buying and selling went on which so offended our Lord. But as most visitors to Paris 'do' Notre-Dame and many new arrivals in London must see Buckingham Palace, so those who came to Jerusalem visited the Temple.

Within that outer court, that was open to all, ran a low stone balustrade which carried a notice forbidding any Gentile to pass beyond it under pain of death. Within was the court of the women, not a place reserved for women only, but the area beyond which women might not go. Within again was the court of the priests, to which only the priesthood was admitted. Here stood the giant altar of unhewn stone, 48 feet square, behind which was the dark, windowless cube known as the Holy of Holies. To this came the High Priest only, and he but once a year, and then only after having undergone the prescribed ceremonial cleansing. Increasing holiness was expressed by increasing remoteness. The greater the degree of holiness, the greater the separation from man.

It was only to be expected that this idea, current in Jewish thought and expressed in their religious architecture, should shape the lives of those who were most earnest about their faith. The gospels give glimpses of a group of men who sought to live a holy life in obedience to this principle of separation. These were the Pharisees and their name meant 'the separated ones'.

The picture drawn of the Pharisee in the parable of the publican and the Pharisee is not a caricature. The Pharisee was not as other men. They might sit loosely to the faith of their fathers but not he. Jewish law required that a man should fast once a year – on the Day of Atonement – but the Pharisee did so twice a week. (It is not a bad thing to have one's physical appetites under control.) Jewish law required that tithes be paid on the fruit of the ground; the Pharisee gave a tenth of all his income. (Again, planned giving is not wrong.) So far as morality was concerned, this man came out well. As another one-time Pharisee observed: 'Touching... the law, blameless' (Philippians 3:6). Yet holiness is not to be equated with morality, though morality is a necessary part of holiness. It is when we set the holiness of the Pharisee side by side with the holiness of Jesus that we see:

> *The little more, how much it is,*
> *The little less, how many miles away.*

The Pharisee was not a bad man, if by that we mean one who is unchaste and intemperate, foul in language and filthy in habits. But the holiness of Jesus was not only the negative grace of sinlessness. Holiness is not a conscious rectitude, a continual watching of my step lest the wrong foot be put forward first. Separation, by itself, is not enough. Holiness is not just not doing things and not going places. I am not made good solely by what I do not do.

Think of Scrooge. He never went to the theatre or haunted low dives, yet no one would call him a holy man. And why? Because there was absent from his life the one particular element that constitutes the very essence of Christian holiness.

What was there in Jesus that was lacking in the average Pharisee? Not the element of morality. That was present and deserves full marks. Not the practice of religious exercises. The Pharisee's dress and conduct made him as conspicuous as a Salvationist in full uniform. But with Jesus there was the quality of love that is the first of the fruits of the Holy Spirit's presence. The ceaseless activity of love as expressed in the life of Jesus is the distinctive element in the Christian experience of holiness. Therefore Christlikeness is holiness. Where Christ is enthroned, there is holiness. Yet holiness is never an 'imitation' of Christ, if by that is meant a self conscious external patterning. Christian holiness will spring from the inward possession of that same Holy Spirit who was in Jesus and by whose power he wrought and taught.

So the blessing of holiness is never an 'it'. No one should say: 'I've got it!', for the experience is personal and the source of the experience is personal. Things and places can never be holy because of any intrinsic virtue that they may be held to possess. There is no holy water save that which is fit for human use. There is no holy ground save in terms of William Cowper's lines:

Jesus, where'er thy people meet,
There they behold the mercy seat;
Where'er they seek thee thou art found,
And every place is hallowed ground.

Is Westminster Cathedral holy but the Regent Hall not? And if either is holy it is only because those who gather there are men and women in whose heart dwells that same Holy Spirit who was in Jesus. The work of the Spirit was perfectly exemplified in Jesus and he can make us like him, not through any outward conformity but by the workings of inward grace.

Finally, if it be asked whether this experience is the work of a moment or a matter of years, the answer is – both. For example, I was commissioned as an officer of The Salvation Army on Monday 3 May 1920. But I have been learning ever since how better to do my work as an officer, and that task is never ending. There will always be some fresh truth to be discovered. Perfection in any full and final sense will never come my way. Ever there will be the glory of going on and still to be.

I can yield my forgiven life to God that he may bestow upon me as much of his Spirit as I am able at that moment to receive. That may take place at a moment of time. But the work of the Holy Spirit in my life will never be ended for it is the greatest of the saints who have been most conscious of their imperfections. Those who live closest to Jesus are most aware of how far they fall short of his glory. Yet that same Holy Spirit who was in him is in them. Their sense of their shortcomings is not due to his absence but to his presence.

Here then is the twofold work of the Spirit. He can purify, but he will reveal what more remains to be purified. He can provoke us to that disinterested service for God and man which is love in action, but he will make us long to serve more selflessly still. His work will never be done, though his first coming may have been at a recognisable moment. Our separateness will not be a separateness from people, but a separation from sin unto God and a dedication to people.

Though the presence of the Holy Spirit does not guarantee immunity from temptation or exemption from failure, he will give us grace to grow:

> *… like him who my pattern shall be,*
> *Till in his beauty my King I shall see.*
> (Eliza E. Hewitt, *The Song Book of*
> *The Salvation Army,* no 443 v4)

Four

The Decisive Experience

*Acts 26:13-19: 'At midday, O king, I saw
in the way a light from heaven… heard a voice
speaking unto me… I was not disobedient.'*

IT is no accident that one story in the Acts of the
Apostles is told three times over – that of the
conversion of Saul of Tarsus.

First of all, the original event is described in
circumstantial detail in chapter nine. This account
can have come only from the apostle himself. Some
20 years later the apostle was repeating the same
story almost word for word, as can be read in
chapter 22, when the mob in the Jerusalem temple
was clamouring for his blood. The third account, in
chapter 26, is part of his trial before Herod Agrippa,
great-grandson of Herod the Great (he of the
Massacre of the Innocents) with Festus in
attendance. On each of these critical occasions the
apostle did not fall back on any legal or theological
arguments – as he could well have done – but chose
to base his defence on his own personal testimony.

Yet though the story of the apostle's conversion is
repeated but three times in the New Testament, it

could have been that he told it many times more on his thousands of miles of missionary journeyings. Told it until his travelling companions almost knew it off by heart, as we sometimes know by heart the story of the conversion of some trophy of grace because we have heard it so frequently. This basic fact emerges in his epistles as well. References are many to the work of God's grace in his own life.

Personal testimony was a basic element in the earliest Christian preaching. Those second- and third-century church fathers – Justin, Irenaeus, Tertullian, Clement, Cyprian – are but names to us and their rather wordy addresses interest few but the student. But they did not fail to include, in greater or lesser detail, some account of their own conversion in what they said. They wrote and spoke from the heart as well as the head.

Many renewals of the Christian faith have been marked by a revival of personal testimony. This was true of the Army's own beginnings. Volume One of our history by Colonel Robert Sandall describes a free and easy meeting on a Sunday afternoon in 1868 that began at three o'clock, lasted 90 minutes, in which 43 people gave a personal witness and parts of eight hymns were sung. Said Catherine Booth, addressing the yearly meeting of the Society of Friends in July 1882: 'The people do not come to hear the preacher as to see the Bills and Dicks... who have been converted, and they come still more to hear them speak.'

Now this matter of personal testimony has its own difficulties for we Salvationists of present generations. We may never have plunged catastrophically into sin. Nor have we ever wasted our substance in riotous living in a far country. We might even feel it to be an exaggeration to describe ourselves as brands plucked from the burning. Most of the commandments have we kept from our youth up. Must our testimony then be less effective than that of our fathers? In other words, must sin abound before an experience of grace can much more abound? As the apostle himself said in another connection: God forbid! (Romans 6:1).

The experience called conversion can express itself in different ways for different people. No two human encounters with the grace of God are ever exactly the same. To some conversion is such a drastic change that it can be described only as in Oliver Cooke's chorus: 'I know a place where night is turned to day.' And that not in a slow dawn where light imperceptibly brightens the sky, but with the suddenness of a lightning flash which illuminates what has hitherto been pitch black.

But to others among us conversion may be more truthfully likened to slow dynamite. We have always believed in such general truths that God is love, that in his mercy sin can be forgiven, and that by his grace temptation can be overcome. These things we have heard from the Primary (Sunday school) onwards. But there comes a moment when these truths to which we have long given passive assent suddenly become compellingly alive. They seize us by the throat. They demand that we live by them. The slow burning fuse, first set alight maybe in the Sunday afternoon company meeting, now reaches the powder barrel and our adolescent sophistications are blown sky high. Saving truth confronts us and demands that we accept as a matter of personal conviction the gospel that we have heard from the days of our childhood.

Outwardly there may be little change in the externals of our living. We wear the same kind of clothes. We continue at the grammar school or with our apprenticeship on the shop floor. Indeed, we have much the same friends and come to the Army hall as often as we came before. But inwardly that moment of illumination and dedication is never to be forgotten. For us the Christian faith has become alive and meaningful.

For comparison, think of how we can be awakened in some unexpected moment to the beauty of the world in which we live. There was a day in the life of Charles Lamb when he visited Wordsworth at Grasmere, then followed the bed of the Lodore Hotel and afterwards the climb to the top of Skiddaw. 'That day,' he wrote, 'will stand out like a mountain in my life.'

Or think of how we can be unexpectedly awakened to the beauty of the language we have always spoken. In his reminiscences, *Sometime*

Never, Wilfred Pickles has described how, as a lad in the Halifax Public Library, he suddenly came across the *Oxford Book of English Poetry*. Time stood still as he succumbed to the magic spell of words. Halifax was forgotten until, moved by a sudden impulse, he hid the book (which he later replaced) beneath his coat and hurriedly left the library.

Then, as a builder's labourer, connecting a drain pipe to a main sewer, he astonished his mate by standing in the trench and reciting from A.E. Housman's 'A Shropshire Lad':

In summertime on Bredon
The bells they sound so clear;
Round both the shires they ring them
In steeples far and near,
A happy noise to hear.

Here of a Sunday morning
My love and I would lie,
And see the coloured counties,
And hear the lark so high
Above us in the sky.

And I would turn and answer
Among the springing thyme,
'Oh, peal upon our wedding,
And we will hear the chime,
And come to church in time.'

They tolled the one bell only,
Groom there was none to see,
The mourners followed after,
And so to church went she,
And would not wait for me.

The bells they sound on Bredon,
And still the steeples hum.
'Come all to church, good people,' –
Oh, noisy bells, be dumb;
I hear you, I will come.

Thereafter to the youthful Wilfred poetry was never a string of meaningless words, the fad of the highbrow, the cult of the aesthete. No more could he escape her magic.

These are but comparisons with that moment of illumination when beliefs passively held become livingly true. We do not need to have been very bad in order, by God's grace, to be made good – though at the crisis point we may doubtless feel bad enough. But while Paul called himself 'the chief of sinners' gross habits had never mastered him. Like the rich young ruler he also had kept the commandments. No coarseness of living had ever soiled his character. He was an earnest, well educated young man who made the great discovery that the acceptance of Jesus as Saviour and Lord answered his mental perplexities and satisfied the deepest needs of his soul. And this is where many of us come in.

For example, what kind of a man penned the familiar lines:

Long my imprisoned spirit lay
Fast bound in sin and nature's night;

He was the son of a clergyman, himself an ordained clergyman, a young man already possessed of a deserved reputation for godliness, who nevertheless on Whit Sunday morning 1738, at the age of 30, wrote that:

My chains fell off, my heart was free,
I rose, went forth, and followed thee.

As with Charles Wesley, the chains that bind us may not be those of the more vicious forms of evil living. We may be held captive by our own timidities and hesitations. Our dungeon may be that of our own fears and misgivings. Self, rather than sinning, may hold us prisoner. But from any and all of these outward signs of inward failure we may be delivered by committing ourselves without reserve to Jesus as Saviour and Lord.

So the new birth may well be that moment when, in an act of penitent self surrender to Christ, the Lord becomes a living reality and his daily presence our all-sufficiency. This is but one of several ways of spelling out our obedience to the familiar command 'Believe on the Lord Jesus Christ, and thou shalt be saved' (Acts 16:31).

Five

They Twain
Shall be One

*Mark 10:9: 'What therefore God hath
joined together, let not man put asunder.'*

AMONG some Salvation Army books I received
was the revised edition of the *General Orders for
Conducting Salvation Army Ceremonies.* Clean and
unmarked, this was in happy contrast to the now
soiled volume which had done me good service over
many years.

But I was unashamedly fond of the old book for
it contained in the margins the names of those
children whom I had dedicated under the Army flag
with the prayer: 'Heavenly Father, take this child,
A.B., to be thine own.' And the names of some of
the saints who had received an abundant entrance
into the heavenly kingdom: 'As it has pleased
Almighty God…' as well as the names of those
young Salvationists whom I had joined in marriage,
asking them to repeat after me: 'I do solemnly
declare that I know not of any lawful impediment
why I, A.B., may not be joined in matrimony to

C.D.' And the new book, like the old, still quotes the text which I have pronounced in blessing more times than I can remember: 'Whom God hath joined together…' This is not a liturgical formula. The phrase did not originate in any church office. These are the words of Jesus which, when first uttered, clinched the teaching he was giving on the essence of marriage.

Discussion about the nature of marriage is no new thing. In the first century, as in the current century, the character of marriage was frequently a matter of public debate. There was no unanimous opinion as to whether there were justifiable grounds – and, if so, what these were – for the termination of marriage. It was in this setting that Jesus proclaimed marriage as a lifelong union. The context shows that to a direct question he gave a direct answer.

As a Christian community we are concerned to practise and to maintain the sacrament of Christian marriage. This does not mean that we regard as less worthy, or any less binding, the vows which may be taken by any two contracting parties before a civil registrar. We also realise that practising Christians are somewhat of a minority and this means we cannot impose our views, however dearly we hold them, upon society if a majority of that society refuses to live by them.

Nevertheless, we are entitled to testify to our convictions. Indeed, we are duty-bound to do so. As citizens of a democracy we have as much right to contend for our convictions as those who think differently from us contend for theirs. We are not to be silenced because our principles are derided as outmoded, square, Victorian, or saddled with any other denigratory epithet which not infrequently takes the place of rational argument. If we cannot coerce the majority, we are not to be coerced by the majority. Within the fellowship of practising Christians it is our concern to see that we follow our Lord in all our relationships. Nowhere is this more essential than in that personal and intimate relationship known as marriage.

Let the starting point be that Christian people will be one in their lifelong affection, for Christian marriage is the lifelong union of husband and wife. And far from this being a harsh or oppressive rule – as is sometimes argued – it is all of a piece with the intention of most young people, including those who sit lightly to organised religion.

Forget the celebrities whose names make headlines in the media. Those unhappy people are not normal themselves, nor is their way of life to be accepted as a norm by others. What lad takes his girl to the altar but on the assumption – unspoken at times but nevertheless deeply cherished – that this is for good and always? And what girl goes to the altar but in the assurance that this is for keeps? She doesn't expect to be discarded, neither to discard. At that moment a pro tem arrangement is neither in their thinking nor their dreaming. If it were, they would not be where they are.

This is where the majority of our young folk begin. Some of our loquacious social theorists fail to pay sufficient attention to this indisputable fact. Certain of them father their own disillusionments with life upon those for whom they claim to speak. But to those young folk who bring their unspoilt ideals to the altar the Christian church says: how right you are. We are with you. This is the Christian way – and we want to help you to keep to it.

How can this ideal be maintained?

Here Christian grace comes to the help of Christian teaching. Oneness in mutual affection can be undergirded by oneness of dedication to God.

We who are Salvationists are at some advantage here. For we are united not only in our devotion to one another but also in our dedication to God. This is the principle that underlies every Salvation Army wedding. This is the reason why, in many instances, the Salvationist bride and bridegroom are married in uniform. Our religion is not a 'one service on a Sunday' affair. Our faith enters into every relationship of life. It enables us to make a discriminating use of our leisure. It guides our conduct in business. It sets the foundations of our home life. And our faith cannot be kept out of our wedding – one of the most crucial moments in any life. If our religion means anything to us at all, it must have some bearing upon our attitude to marriage. If it can be ignored here, it can be ignored anywhere. If it is dismissed as irrelevant here, it is irrelevant everywhere. But for us our devotion to one another is expressed within the context of our dedication to God.

This point does not need to be laboured to those who have before them the example of William and Catherine Booth. It would be impossible to tell the story of one without frequent reference to the other.

This is not always true of great religious figures. For example, the 95 Theses attached to the door of the Castle Church at Wittenberg on the eve of All Saints' Day 1517 owed nothing to any woman. Luther had crossed his Rubicon before ever he married Catherine von Bora. Upon his public life (said one biographer) the influence of his marriage cannot be traced.

The unwearying journeys of John Wesley in the 18th century owed little, if anything, to Mary Vazeille. He would have criss crossed England with equal energy had he never married.

Not so with William and Catherine. To decide (wrote Laura Petri) whether William or Catherine Booth was the founder of The Salvation Army is to venture on the speculation whether the child derives its being from father or from mother. The Army was started not with one motor but with two.

The unity of devotion and dedication is to be seen not in one illustrious couple only but in many. Not only – for example – in Salvation Army leaders such as Edward and Catherine Higgins, or Leonard and Margaret Woodward, or John and Jenny Murfitt, but I see this unity of dedication strengthening a unity of devotion every time I see a photograph of a young Army bride and bridegroom. I see this unity going from strength to strength in the Salvationist husband and wife who serve in their home corps with their children following happily in their footsteps. And I see this unity at its finest hour as, for example, in reports in *The War Cry* where the *Huddersfield Examiner* featured two veteran Salvationists, with more than a century of service between them, who still sell Salvation Army papers from public house to public house and who, despite their age or, probably, because of their age, devote themselves unweariedly to the youth activities of the corps.

And when we inquire still further into this matter, we discover that this unity of devotion, expressed in a unity of dedication, is sustained by a unity of supplication. Two people live together. They serve God and man together. They pray together.

My word to all Salvationists is that in this matter they should begin as they mean to go on. There is no reason why a lad and a girl who are going steady should not share their prayers as well as their plans. And when two people set up house together, it should be as natural for them to pray together as to eat together. This does not mean that they will not want to pray separately. We all have matters on our heart about which we pray each for himself, but a Bible reading and a prayer at the most convenient time of day should be as much a part of the domestic routine as washing the dishes. And if there is company to the meal at which it is customary to hold such a short act of family worship, none need hesitate to say to the visitors: 'I hope you won't mind joining us in our prayers' – and then go on as if it were as natural as pouring out a second cup of tea.

Those who have read *Triumph of Faith* will know that the late Bandmaster George Marshall and his wife, Jenny, had made a habit of praying together once a day ever since their wedding and, as an extra, George would repeat Psalm 23.

In the early hours of a January morning, shortly before his promotion to Glory, the Bandmaster woke up under the impression that they had forgotten to pray as was their custom before retiring.

'Of course we prayed,' said Jenny. George Marshall was not entirely convinced. 'Let's go through the 23rd Psalm again,' he replied.

So this devoted husband and wife repeated: 'The Lord is my shepherd. Yea, though I walk through the valley of the shadow of death, I will fear no evil: for thou art with me…'

To pray together is to be shielded from evil, not only from the perils that beset the body but also from the dangers that assail the soul.

Like all other Christian relationships, Christian marriage calls for Christian grace. We cannot obey the commands of Jesus without the help of Jesus. But that help, when sought, is never denied. Nor will it be refused to any who seek the happiness of the home of which Christ is the head.

Six

Secular and Sacred

(given at Woolwich Parish Church)
Romans 12:1: 'I beseech you therefore, brethren,
by the mercies of God, that ye present your bodies
a living sacrifice, holy, acceptable unto God,
which is your reasonable service.'

ANY here present who have visited Christ Church in the Blackfriars Road will know that some years ago there was dedicated a set of stained glass windows representing life and work in the borough of Southwark, depicting – among others – dockside workers, a baker, a mother and her children, a butcher and an office cleaner. Mrs Mopp 'old style', with voluminous skirt, hair in a kind of turban, armed with a broom, is set beside Mrs Mopp 'new style', with perm and set, gold watch on wrist, kneeling beside her bucket.

The cynic might dismiss this as another kind of ecclesiastical gimmick and argue that Mrs Mopp owes a greater debt to the late Mr Thomas Handley than to the church. But I am prepared to contend in all seriousness that for her recognition in the Christian roll of honour there is sound historical and theological warrant.

Certainly historical – for the visitor to some of the more ancient churches which line the coast of my native county of Fife, will see hanging from the roof beams replicas of the tools used by the local fishermen in their calling. To bring work and religion, religion and work, together in a holy calling is not a bright idea of the current century. This conception of the wholeness of life has its roots in the Old Testament.

And theological – for this call to present to God our bodies refers, primarily, to this body by means of which I have my being and earn my living. Which is another way of saying that divine service is not limited to a particular hour on a Sunday morning or Sunday evening, but covers all that takes place both in my 40 hour week as well as in my hours of leisure. The purpose of the Christian faith is needlessly curtailed if its application is limited to special times and special areas of life. The redemptive purpose of God is as concerned with the way in which a man uses his time and spends his money as the way in which he says his prayers.

'I thank thee, O Father, Lord of Heaven and earth…' said Jesus, as he spoke of the way in which the proud rejected him but the humble welcomed him. This was as if he had said, 'I thank thee, O Father, Lord of church and factory,' or 'Lord of pew and pit,' or 'Lord of worship and work'.

Our Lord was rejecting, once and for all, the thought that there were areas of life where the writ of his Father did not run. We all know that there is a plain difference between a place of worship and an industrial plant, though the balance of life requires our attendance at both. But to suppose that what goes on in the one – but not the other – is of interest to God, is to put paid to true religion and to deprive man of his only hope of a salvation which can redeem the whole of his life.

If, like me, you have grown up children, you will see them variously occupied. So I see my eldest daughter bringing up her family, with those round the clock demands which family life makes and, as I watch her, I say to myself: this is divine service. It is divine service when she is busy making their dinner as it is when she is hearing them say their prayers. If it is not divine service – and every young mother will echo this question – what on earth is she doing with her time and brains and energy? And as I see another of my family – as I did in the autumn of 1964 – leading 200 boys and 100 girls in a Salvation Army secondary school in eastern Nigeria in an act of morning worship before lessons begin for the day, then I say that this is also divine service. Indeed, the only service that is not divine is the wretched commercialisation of human weaknesses by which the unscrupulous among us live handsomely on the sad failings of their fellows.

But the shoe repairer who helps to keep people's feet dry, the shopkeeper who serves wholesome food over his counter, the garage mechanic whose repair job is utterly dependable – and all others like them

– can present their bodies, that is to say, what they do, to God as their acceptable service.

In this connection I recall a civil servant friend of mine who was, and is, a Salvationist, describing how a senior government official came up to him one day and said: 'I'm having a house built and the builder is making a good job of it. I look round most nights to see how things are going and the work is first class; nothing skimped or shoddy. The builder's one of your crowd.' There was a man the work of whose body was 'acceptable unto God' and, because acceptable to God, acceptable also to man.

In the second place, we are to present to God not only what the body does but what the body is. We would miss an important part of the meaning of this command if we limited it to our physical and mental activities.

For what is the body intended to be? The temple of the Holy Spirit is the Christian answer. The body is more than a structure of flesh and bones. In this sense the body means the whole personality. 'Your very selves,' translates the *New English Bible* (Romans 12:1). This self or personality, presented to God, can be the temple or home of his Spirit, thus becoming yet another human instrument which God can use to accomplish his will on earth.

Keeping this truth in mind, it becomes plainer still that the outworking of the Holy Spirit of God cannot be limited to one particular day of the week, much less to particular hours on a particular day.

The man whose body has thus been presented to God will find that his life makes its own continuous witness seven days a week. As H. M. Stanley said of David Livingstone when they finally parted: 'Religion made him the most companionable of men... he preached no sermon by word of mouth while I was in his company, but each day witnessed a sermon acted.'

It may be thought the height of unsophistication to quote:

We are the only Bible
A careless world will read;
We are the sinner's gospel,
We are the scoffer's creed.

But, naive or not, we are living epistles. We are being read, whether we care for it or not. And it is by what men see in those who name the name of Christ that the Kingdom of God has been – and will still be – most powerfully advanced. Let T. W. Manson speak to this: 'The Christianity that conquered the Roman Empire was not an affair of brilliant preachers addressing large congregations... When we try to picture how it was done we see domestic servants teaching Christ in and through their domestic service, workers doing it through their work, small shopkeepers through their trade, and so on.' They had presented their bodies to God, and this was the happy result.

Finally, it may be asked why should any layman take his religion so much in earnest? Cannot so thorough-going a committal be left to clergy or ministers while he, who has to work for his living, gets on with the difficult enough task of keeping a roof over the head of himself and his family?

But to whom was – and is – the New Testament addressed? Not just to those who are professionally involved in the Christian cause, but to all the people of God. And it is we – the total people of God, ministers and layfolk alike – who, recognising the immensity of the mercies of God (which please remember were crowned with the gift of Jesus as Saviour), will therefore recognise that this response to him, with the consequent dedication to the needs of men, is our reasonable service.

The operative word here is 'reasonable'. 'An act of intelligent worship,' translates J. B. Phillips. 'This is your rational worship,' says Goodspeed. 'The worship due from you as rational creatures,' wrote Ronald Knox.

The divine appeal is not a sledgehammer planned to stun our bemused intellect into a numbed assent. God is not seeking the cringing response of some servile creature who does as he is told lest a worse thing befall him. He awaits the free response of the free man who, acknowledging the compulsive power of the divine mercies, answers with a clear head and a willing heart.

It was Charles Wesley who, in one of his great

communion hymns, described this total commitment to the will of God in daily living as involving body, mind and soul and consequently, in turn, enriching them all.

Take my soul and body's powers,
Take my memory, mind and will,
All my goods and all my hours,
All I know and all I feel,
All I think or speak or do...
(SASB, no 492 v2)

This is what holy living means – the dedication of as much as I possess to as much as I know of the will of God for me. And far from this total response cramping any man's style, it ennobles him who makes it and glorifies the God whose service is always perfect freedom.

Seven

A 'Christian' Christian

1 John 3:18: 'Let us not love in word,
neither in tongue; but in deed and in truth.'

I RECEIVED from a guest residing in one of our eventide homes a letter that concluded: 'I like our officer here. She is a real Christian Christian.'

A 'Christian' Christian. The phrase expressed not only my concern but my prayer. Let Christians be Christian!

Hardly a day passes but someone, with or without knowledge, discourses upon the failure of the Church. For this alleged failure differing reasons are adduced. Usually some fault of organisation or method is held to be responsible for the present inadequacy of organised religion. But as I listen to these discussions I am reminded of the question addressed to Goethe in his day:

'What drives poetry out of the world?'

'Poets!' was his answer.

If the Christian faith is finally on its way out – which assumption I deny – what could have reduced it to such impotence and robbed it of its life changing effectiveness?

Christians – must be the answer.

For sadly it has to be said that there are some believers who are the worst enemies of their own cause. The faith that we hold will not be destroyed by the assaults of its foes. Indeed, as I see in the media the attacks made upon the Christian faith, I am almost comforted. Is this shying at an Aunt Sally all we have to fear? For this figure of straw, set up by some of our assailants for the express purpose of knocking it down, is often a travesty of the faith, bearing little resemblance to its true nature and power.

In any case, we who are believers should remember that it is nothing new for the Christian faith to be reviled and its adherents harried out of their lives. This has been part of the history of the Church from the beginning. Knowing our Acts of the Apostles we have not forgotten the stoning of Stephen, nor the death of James by the sword, nor the attempted lynching of the apostle Paul within the precincts of the Jerusalem temple, nor the banishment of the aged John to Patmos. And if it is the war of words that we fear, the most savage attack today is mild compared, for example, with the pretty line in invective practised by the second century pagan philosopher Celsus, one of whose mildest remarks was to compare believers to frogs croaking in a swamp.

But these are not the folk we have to fear, whether their abuse be verbal or physical. As

Theodore Beza said to the King of Navarre after the Massacre of Vassy: 'Sire, it is in truth the lot of the Church… to endure blows and not to strike them. But also may it please you to remember that it is an anvil which has worn out many hammers.'

My concern has not to do so much with the attacks made upon our faith from without as with its betrayals from within. The promise is that the gates of Hell shall not prevail against the Church of God, and on that promise we can rely. But it is when Christians are less than Christian that the citadel is opened from within to an enemy who, left to his own stratagems and devices, could never capture it from without.

My concern is therefore threefold.

1) *Let us be Christian in our relationships with one another* – for surely charity begins at home.

I find myself free to pursue this line of thought for it is a standing rule with The Salvation Army never to criticise either the conduct, the mode of worship, or the administrative structure of any other church. A research student could go through our press files for the century-plus of our existence and look in vain for any unfriendly comment upon our fellow Christians, either in their individual behaviour or corporate worship.

This is not because the Army itself was never criticised, for it was – unmercifully at times, and by some who regarded themselves as doing the Lord's work. But 'better suffer than contend' was the rule of William Booth, and his heirs and assigners seek to follow his example.

So I can with a clear conscience express my regret at some of the infighting that still takes place within the Christian ranks today.

Examples are not hard to come by. There are those who see no value in a Billy Graham-style Earls Court campaign, and there are others who regard Rome as a child of Hell. There are those who refuse the grace of God permission to flow through any ecclesiastical channel save their own, and there are others who look askance upon any Christian fellowship that may rise above denominational barriers.

Now these varying opinions may be sincerely held. What is amiss is when those who hold them excommunicate with bell, book and candle all who do not. And lest it be supposed that I have a particular person or group of persons in mind, let me say with sadness that this form of intolerance – and its twin brother, self-righteousness – is not limited to any particular school of thought. I have sampled them at both ends of the theological spectrum.

Could it be that we all need to look again at the reply of our Lord when John said to him in Luke 9:49: 'Master, we saw one casting out devils in thy name; and we forbad him, because he followeth not with us'? 'Jesus said unto him, forbid him not: for he that is not against us is for us' (Luke 9:50).

Let us rather thank God that he fulfils himself in many ways. He can speak through a ritual hallowed by centuries of usage and he can speak through the street corner open-air meeting. He can speak through the cathedral anthem and he can speak through the gospel chorus. He can speak through Johann Sebastian Bach and he can speak through the Joystrings [a Salvation Army pop group of the 1960s]. He can speak through the priest upon whom episcopal hands have been laid and he can speak through the testimony of the layman whose heart is the Lord's.

I drive this nail home (I hope) with some sentences from one of the wisest of all spiritual teachers The Salvation Army has known – Samuel Brengle: 'The Spirit filled man is tolerant of those who differ from him in opinion or doctrine… He is firm in his own convictions… but he does not condemn and consign to damnation all those who differ from him… And as I grow older my faith becomes more simple. What a mistake so to crowd one's faith with furniture that there is hardly any room for folk.'

And it is folk, not furniture, who matter.

2) *But let us also be Christian in our attitude to the world about us* – and that world can be defined as society organised apart from God.

This means that with some aspects of the life of the world, the believer will have nothing whatever to do. On every count he will dissociate himself from its commercialism, remembering the Master's teaching that a man's life consisteth not in the abundance of the things which he possesseth (Luke 12:15). Nor will he share in its self seeking, again remembering that Jesus said that he who would save his life shall lose it (Matthew 16:25 or Luke 9:24). Nor, as grace shall be given him, will he share its sinfulness.

Now these sharp distinctions may sound an unwelcome departure in tone from that understanding and acceptance of one another for which these sentences were earlier pleading.

In the relationships of believers one with another, let it be said that the closer our walk with God, the closer our walk with each other, but also the less shall we find in common with those who do not share that closer walk. Indeed, my experience is that those who make no profession of faith are more than a shade surprised should our ways too closely resemble theirs. If they do, what's the difference between us? Why harp on about the need for salvation if the resulting distinction is minimal?

A mordant cartoon once appeared in *Punch* of a padre rising from table at an officers' mess and, as he disappeared through the door, leaving behind him the stale smell of a story too close to the bone, the Colonel was saying, 'What I can't stand is this unholier than thou attitude.'

Yet though there is bound to be an unmistakable difference between the man who belongs to Christ and the man who does not, that gulf should be bridged from our side by our desire for his salvation and for that of the world to which he belongs. After all, God does not hate the world. How can he hate that which is his own creation? Nor has he given the world up as if it were past praying for. He has provided some better thing for it.

'For God sent not his Son into the world to condemn the world; but that the world through him might be saved' (John 3:17). And with unwearying patience we who are believers must labour, as did our Lord before us, for the salvation of the world for which he died. Our methods, our approaches may vary. Thank God they do. But the same spirit will animate us and the same goal will unite us. And as the object of divine love is 'the world', the salvation of Saigon will matter as much as that of Sunderland or Seattle, and that of Hanoi as much as Hull or Halifax or Houston.

3) *To live after this pattern presupposes that we are Christian in spirit.*

This is our basic need – to commit ourselves so unreservedly to Christ that we may receive of the spirit of Christ. That is to say, we cannot effectively proclaim Christ as Saviour to others unless we personally know him as such ourselves.

One thing is clear, a nominal Christianity is of little use today. The formalities of religion avail nothing either to the believer or to the cause. A nominal Christianity is a contradiction in terms.

The man who is Christian in name only is more of a hindrance than a help. No man can truly be Christ's only in name. 'If any man have not the Spirit of Christ, he is none of his' (Romans 8:9). A Christianity that is merely nominal is powerless to stand against the forces of secularism. Lacking any inner life of its own, it will capitulate to an enemy that, though irreligious in name, possesses all the dynamic of a religion.

So my last and greatest concern is that all of us who bear the name of Christ shall live by the power of Christ because he, who lived and died and rose again, lives by faith in our hearts.

Eight

Salute to the Founder

*Acts 26:16: 'I have appeared unto thee for
this purpose, to make thee a minister and a witness.'*

ON 26 June 1907, the Regius Professor of Civil Law
presented to convocation – the Chancellor, the Rt
Hon Lord Curzon of Kedleston, presiding – 'certain
distinguished persons' to receive the degree of
Doctor of Civil Law, the 22nd of whom was listed as
'The Rev William Booth, Founder and Commander
in Chief of The Salvation Army.'

Quoting from the *Aeneid*, from the conversation
in the underworld between Anchises and Aeneas, Dr
Goudy said that the work of William Booth had
been to seek out his fellow creatures *clausi tenebris et
carcere caeco* (hedged in by dark and blind
environment) 'in order to lure to brighter worlds
and lead the way.'

Such a generous judgement would not be for a
moment questioned by any Salvationist, so long as it
is remembered that the 'brighter worlds' of
Goldsmith's parson in 'The Deserted Village'
include what God has promised to those who love
him both here and hereafter. Nor would this

judgement be questioned by the public generally. For though William Booth encountered no small hostility at various times in his long life, he also won the respect of men who came from very different backgrounds and who held very different attitudes to life from his own.

I can recall, for example, that when Middleton Murry was launching *The Adelphi* soon after the First World War, an early issue of that magazine carried a very sympathetic account of the Founder preaching in the city of Oxford. And beside that I set a much earlier appreciation by Cardinal Manning when William Booth had sent him a copy of *In Darkest England and the Way Out*. 'It fully commands my sympathy,' wrote the Cardinal. 'Every living soul costs the most precious blood, and we ought to save it, even the worthless and the worst.'

But if there were at one time some who would have stoned William Booth, the present danger is that he be canonised and the cutting edge of his deeds and words be blunted by the dead weight of the larger than life monument that we raise to his honour. It would be ironic – which may God avert! – if this soldier-prophet became a piece of Victoriana, an historical curiosity who, having served his day, fell on sleep, which example it is suggested by some that his soldiers would do well to copy.

That this is no hypothetical danger comes

home to me every time a reporter or interviewer leads off with the remark that the social conditions which galvanised William Booth into action have disappeared from our common life. Must not The Salvation Army that he founded be therefore something of a Victorian anachronism and should it not, like its Founder, now pass from the scene of action?

In reply two comments should be made.

The first is that it is quite true that the obvious mass poverty which disgraced the mid 19th century has disappeared. When William Booth, just out of his teens, first came to London after a year's unemployment in his native city of Nottingham, C. J. Blomfield, then Bishop of London, could speak of 'the immense population within a mile or a mile and a half to the east and north east of St Paul's living in a most wretched state of destitution and neglect'.

But while such mass poverty is no more, let it not be supposed that our land is now free from poverty. There is time for one fact only from the report entitled *Homeless Single Persons*, published by Her Majesty's Stationery Office in November 1966. A census revealed their number to be just under 30,000 and of this number The Salvation Army will sleep tonight – and every night – a minimum of 7,500, being (as the report states) the largest single provider, at the lowest charge for food and shelter, of accommodation for the homeless in this country (UK). There is need for a renewed awakening of the social conscience of our land concerning continuing poverty in the midst of comparative plenty.

But my second point is this – suppose our community needs were fully met, who says that it was these which first moved William Booth to action? Not he himself; nor his several biographers. Moved to action by spiritual poverty – yes. The other followed after. 'All our social service,' was his oft repeated remark, 'is the outcome of the spiritual life of our people.'

It was the spiritual needs of men and women which made the first – and the last – claim upon his great heart. His ordination was to be 'a minister and a witness' to turn men 'from darkness to light, and from the power of Satan unto God, that they may receive forgiveness of sins, and inheritance among them which are sanctified' (Acts 26:16,18). Were this land a social paradise, there would still be need for this spirit of apostolic adventure – perhaps even more so because men, having food and raiment, might therewith be the more easily content.

William Booth knew this well enough. There is a story of him riding along with a government minister of one of the Australian colonies who sought to improve the occasion by referring to a friend who owned so many thousand head of cattle and so many tens of thousands of sheep. Whereat the Founder looked the minister in the eye and said:

'It takes a good many sheep to satisfy a soul.' 'I suppose you're right,' was the mumbled reply.

It might be thought that Aneurin Bevan and William Booth make strange bedfellows, but the Founder would undoubtedly have agreed with the sentence which was a favourite quote of Mr Bevan: 'A society which limits its idea of civilisation to the accumulation of material abundance, and of justice to their equitable distribution among its members, will never make of its cities anything that differs in essence from a group of anthills.' This is but to say in many words what our Lord said in a few: 'A man's life consisteth not in the abundance of the things which he possesseth' (Luke 12:15).

The obligation to turn men from this darkness to the light rests not upon them but on us. Error will not correct itself. Lost sheep do not return to the fold of their own accord. The lost coin could not find itself. The owner had to sweep diligently until she found it. The man who is outside the Kingdom of God does not wander in by chance. He has to be sought in the highways and byways. If he follows his own bent he will only wander still further into the far country.

I recall now travelling along a dirt road in the outback in New South Wales (Australia) and overtaking a solitary sheep whose fleece was thickly coated with brown dust and knotted with thorns. The creature was plainly lost, but with its head down it was trotting on uphill in a most determined way, but every step a step in the wrong direction. Sheep, coins and men cannot find themselves. They have to be found. And upon us who have accepted Jesus as Saviour and Lord there rests the perpetual obligation to share his redeeming ministry. To this task he still calls us.

It was Jesus who spoke in this way to Paul. 'I have appeared unto thee for this purpose...' (Acts 26:16). It was Jesus who spoke in this way to William Booth. And it is the same Lord who speaks to us in this same way today. He still gives his orders. 'Rise, and stand upon thy feet.' Let no one resent them. For if he cannot command us who are saved by his grace, whom can he command? And if we are not his soldiers to obey, whose orders are we willing to accept in lieu of his?

So far as the Christian gospel is concerned, this is what could be called the crunch. Even those who would reduce our knowledge of the historic Jesus to a minimum leave untouched the fact that he was the friend of publicans and sinners That is to say, his ministry was a redeeming one. Now the work he has for us to do today is none other than the continuance of his own work in the days of his flesh. If his was a gospel of redemption, so must ours be. To preach any other gospel is, as the apostle said elsewhere, to be accursed (Galatians 1:8-9).

But we are not left to attempt this on our own. We are neither thrown back on our own devices nor left to think up our own conception of what our work should be. As his work on earth was a redeeming work, so must ours be also. But, confronted by such a call, none need hesitate. For those who are willing to follow his example will find that the grace of his presence will be all-sufficient.

Nine
The Faith that Saves

Mark 10:52: 'Jesus said... Go thy way;
thy faith hath made thee whole.'

THIS word addressed to Bartimaeus, who sat by the wayside begging, was an oft repeated saying of Jesus. More than once those who came to him for healing left with this reassuring promise bringing peace to heart and mind. It was so with the woman who '...had spent all her living upon physicians, neither could be healed of any' (Luke 8:43), and with the leper of Samaria who was the only one of 10 men in misfortune to return to Jesus to give thanks. And though on other occasions these exact words were not used, the meaning was so close as to make no difference – as when Jesus said to the woman in the house of Simon the Pharisee: 'Thy faith hath saved thee' (Luke 7:50).

What then is this 'faith' that can effect so revolutionary a change in human life? More than a century ago the Army Mother – if I say delivered her soul, that would be inadequate – delivered her mind and soul on this very matter in an address entitled 'A true and a false faith.'

65

I follow in her steps by saying that the faith that saves is not merely a description of the Christian religion as, for example, 'the faith… once delivered unto the saints', where the word stands for a body of doctrine. Articles of faith can be learned by heart and repeated in public worship Sunday by Sunday, without ever becoming the power of God unto salvation.

Nor is the faith that saves to be equated with the small boy's definition of faith as believing what you know ain't true. Nor with the more sophisticated suggestion that faith is believing what you cannot prove.

For faith does not stand by itself. Its purpose and power lie in the object or person in whom that faith reposes. Faith misdirected – that is to say, faith in some nostrum or superstition – can do more harm than good. It then becomes credulity and not faith. And faith is most misdirected of all when it becomes man's trust in himself to choose and see his own path through life and death. This belief of man in man is unbelief in God. His saving help is no longer regarded as necessary. As Karl Barth has said: 'Unbelief is always man's faith in himself.' But the faith that saves can be defined as that trust in God that leads to obedience to God.

Two observations can now be made.

The first is that the faith that saves is not faith in a proposition but faith in a person. For example, in an African classroom in a Salvation Army secondary school that I visited, the blackboard showed that the boys were being taught that the sum of the three angles in any triangle was 180 degrees. This they accepted without dispute. Some may have even memorised the reasoning leading to this conclusion without fully understanding it. They believed it, though it made no difference to their way of life.

I turned from the blackboard to the European Salvation Army officer teacher at her desk and recalled what turbulent tides of nationalism and racialism were threatening the slender bridge of understanding between black and white which she was helping to build. They believe in her, I was told. Now that belief did make a difference to the lads in that class. However cagily those young men may have looked at anyone else not of their race, they believed in that middle aged woman Salvationist.

It is faith in a person that saves. Though, as with our friends, we may be hard put to say in so many words exactly why we believe in a particular person, knowledge has something to do with it, for we do not give a blank cheque to a total stranger. Yet though we may not know all there is to be known about that person, we have learned enough to trust him. We have seen him under pressure and know he does not panic. We have compared his deeds with his words long enough to regard him as a man of integrity. We feel in our bones that what we do know of him so guarantees what we do not yet know that we can fully and freely confide in him.

Now the faith that saves is based first of all on what we know of God. Not that we know everything there is to know about him. Were that so we would be his equal – which is absurd. We know in part. But the part we do know is sufficient, as the Scriptures say, to make us wise unto salvation. God has allowed us to see in Jesus enough of his eternal love and power to make it possible for us to have faith in him.

Here in Christ is a window into the divine nature. 'He that hath seen me hath seen the Father' (John 14:9). And if the love and patience and wisdom and helpfulness which Jesus showed to men in need is a sample of the divine love and patience and wisdom and helpfulness, then that should be sufficient warranty for any man. We can trust a God who is like Jesus. Saving faith does not say I know what I have believed, but I know whom I have believed. We are asked to believe in the saving power of the God and Father of our Lord Jesus Christ.

The second observation is that the faith which saves not only includes the recognition that God can be trusted but requires from those who would trust him the response of obedience. Saving faith has already been defined as that trust in God which leads to obedience to God.

This was one of the oft repeated points made by that queen among theologians – the Army Mother. For what it is worth, I have long been intrigued by her anticipation of what are regarded in certain quarters as the latest insights of theology on this very point.

Here, for example, is Emil Brunner saying: 'Faith is obedience; nothing else.' And here is Bultmann saying: 'Faith is not mere cognisance of Christian truth... but genuine obedience to it.' 'The notion that commitment plays an essential part in religious faith,' declared the Dean of Jesus College in the annual Cambridge Open Lectures for 1964, 'is one of the factors which has greatly influenced contemporary theology.'

Here is Catherine Booth saying in a volume of her addresses, *Life and Death*, published in November, 1883: 'Saving faith is... committal, the giving of... the whole being up to God... just as a young woman when she marries commits herself to her husband... becomes one in spirit with him and has no separate interest henceforth for ever.'

Faith, she said in another address at the same time, is 'that living, powerful, transforming principle in the soul of the believer which enables him to live in obedience to God.'

These words allow me to make a twofold plea.

First of all to those who have not yet accepted Jesus as Saviour. You can trust the God who has revealed himself in Jesus to meet your deepest need. Most probably that need is for forgiveness and cleansing from the guilt and power of sin. These may sound old fashioned phrases but they speak to present need. You can commit yourself without reserve to the God whose word in Christ is: 'Him that cometh unto me I will in no wise cast out' (John 6:37).

There is no need for anyone to doubt this word – as some of our sophisticates do. 'I wish it were true,' said Theodore Dreiser, 'that there was someone to whom a man in his misery might turn... someone of whom the declaration, "Come unto me... and I will give you rest", were true.' To which the answer is that no man need rely upon another man's testimony. Every man can find out for himself whether God is as good as his word.

Then those who have accepted Jesus as Saviour should remember the Army Mother's words that faith will lead not merely to that single act of obedience which brought about your salvation but 'to live in obedience to him'.

Article nine of our doctrines states that 'continuance in a state of salvation depends upon continued obedient faith in Christ'. Is ours continued obedient faith? For we do imperil our salvation if we fail to respond to any further word of command which may reach us from the Lord who is our Saviour. If faith is the trusting of one's sinful life to God for salvation, it is also the trustful dedication of one's redeemed life in obedient service to him. And it is perhaps at this point that the word of truth searches many hearts most deeply.

It is not for me to try to suggest what God in Christ is saying to you. It is for me to ask you to listen and obey. Faith always says yes to Jesus.

Ten

Through a Glass Darkly

(given at an officers' meeting)
Exodus 33:23: 'My face shall not be seen.'

ONE of the rich by-products of Bible study is the light thus thrown upon those problems of leadership which beset us all. One such real-life situation is to be found in the dialogue that occupies the latter part of Exodus chapter 32, and that follows the story of the golden calf.

Despite their backsliding – a reversion to a form of Egyptian worship – Israel was still expected to possess the land of promise. Shaken by this revelation of the brittleness of his people, Moses pleaded the need of additional help whether human or divine is not quite clear from verse 12; maybe he hoped for both.

'Thou hast not let me know whom thou wilt send with me. Yet… this nation is thy people,' he reminded the Lord. For answer he received the promise, 'My presence shall go with thee' (Exodus 33:14).

The heart of the lonely leader rejoiced. All things would yet work together for good. There would be another upon whom he could cast his burdens and, greatly encouraged, Moses dared to ask a yet greater favour: 'I beseech thee, show me thy glory.' That is to say: let me see your face. I would see all and know all.

This was asking a hard thing and, as the subsequent dialogue makes clear, an inexpedient thing. No man has seen God as he is at any time. The exceeding brightness of his presence has always been veiled. His glory to Israel had always been hidden 'in a cloud'. Just as no man can gaze upon the sun – even in eclipse – with his naked eye without doing damage to his sight, so to look upon the undiminished splendour of God (as 414 in our own song book quotes Thomas Binney) is something for which the holiest of mortal men is not ready this side of the grave. Even on the Mount of Transfiguration God spoke out of a cloud. Just the sound of his voice was enough to make the disciples afraid. Though Peter, James and John saw the Son transfigured, the majesty of the Father was mercifully veiled.

So the answer to Moses was 'no'. But not an unqualified 'no'. He would be given sufficient assurance of the might and mercy of God while he was covered by the divine hand 'in the cleft of the rock.' This is a description of a spiritual experience that, because it deals with ultimate realities, is beyond adequate description. Nevertheless, thanks to Augustus Toplady and Fanny Crosby, the phrase has become a word picture of the graciousness of God.

But what Moses asked for – 'thy face', the undimmed glory of the Eternal – was denied him, and denied him for his good. Instead, God gave him as full a revelation of his nature as was needed to sustain him in his task of leadership. Moses glimpsed once again the sovereign uncaused grace and mercy of God. 'I… will be gracious to whom I will be gracious, and will show mercy on whom I will show mercy.' With that Moses had to be content – and with that he could well be content.

What this passage is saying is that alongside every revelation there is always mystery. God everlastingly remains greater than we can know. His ways are always higher than our ways and his thoughts than our thoughts. As Tersteegen observed, 'a God comprehended is no God'. No man, whatever his ecclesiastical authority, knows all the answers about God or about life. Our best judgements are subject to the limitations both of our factual knowledge and of our spiritual discernment. Over every assessment we are compelled to write 'E. & O. E.' (errors and omissions excepted). The most inspired of God's servants can know only in part and can prophesy only in part. In our moments of greatest certainty, when we are most sure that our own actions are right and that our judgement of the actions of other people is doubly right, we have to remind ourselves, with Paul, that we see through a glass, darkly.

The rabbis had a legend that Moses saw God through a window of horn, and there are commentators who see an allusion to this in the apostle's phrase. Be this correct or not, the truth remains that though revelation be granted, mystery abides. Revelation and mystery, like light and darkness, day and night, keep company together. They depend upon each other for their existence and significance. This being so, we can hardly quarrel with life as God made it. Like Carlyle's lady who agreed to accept the universe, we can but do the same. We know – but we know only in part. We see through a glass darkly – but still we see. Whether we like it or not, this is how life deals with us, which is much the same as saying that this is how God deals with us.

As leaders, with the responsibilities of our office, this truth has a bearing on what happens to us and on what happens within us.

Taking the first of these two points, it is no exaggeration to say that most Salvation Army biographers – ancient and modern – contain a paragraph or a page where the officer concerned wonders why this and not that has befallen him, or why he is at X and not Y.

To begin with ancient – that is to say, within the short space of the 20th century – in *Notable Officers of The Salvation Army* Mrs General Carpenter has told the story of Captain (later Commissioner) David Rees being moved, without a word of explanation, from congregations of thousands and converts by the hundreds to a village corps. The newcomer explored the district in very short time and found one church, two chapels, and the tiny room that was his hall, to serve the spiritual needs of a population which was less than the largest of his former congregations. Rees went to his knees, as well he might, for there is no other place where a man can go in such a case.

Now it must be that the hand of God is in what are written off as the mistakes of men else he would be shut out of a large part of life. Or, if there be reservations about such a statement, is it not true that all our actions – wise and unwise, perfect and faulty, conceived in love or tinged with spleen – take place within the framework of God's providence? By this is meant not only the general providence that is rooted in his love for his creation, but that particular providence that has to do with our individual lives. If he has the whole world in his hands, then he must have each of us in his hands as well. The greater includes the less.

Theoretically we may agree but in practice be slow to accept. 'It seemed to him,' wrote Patrick White in *Riders in the Chariot* of the dying Jew, Himmelfarb, 'as though the mystery of failure might be pierced only by those of extreme simplicity of soul, or by one who was about to doff the outgrown garment of the body.'

With such 'extreme simplicity of soul' David Rees resolved that, as God had called him to be an officer, he would never leave that calling. Further, having accepted the government of the Army as God's order for his life, he could never be sent to the wrong place. Finally, wherever he was sent he would make the most of available opportunities. 'At this desert corps' (Mrs Carpenter's phrase) he laid the foundation of his intimate knowledge of the Bible.

As for a modern instance, on page 137 of *The House of my Pilgrimage* General Albert Orsborn wrote of a time when '… my circumstances as an officer were clouded with misunderstanding. The fares of my family to Canada would be paid, and there was a church appointment waiting for me, where I would be near my parents and brothers. I could make out a convincing case for resigning. Twelve good men and true would undoubtedly have given me the same verdict.'

Such honesty illustrates the truth that we cannot expect to be God's favoured children just because we stand in a special relationship to him. Any theologian knows that scriptural election is never election to privilege but to duty. The fact that my all is on the altar does not exempt me from the disappointments and frustrations to which all flesh is heir.

There are those who speak of 'being frustrated' as if this were an experience peculiar to Salvation Army life. Any who so think should read the memoirs of Lord Chandos in which he describes how he was nominated or appointed – only for the British Prime Minister, Sir Winston Churchill, to change his mind – to nine leading offices in the Commonwealth including Secretary of State for War (twice), Ambassador to Washington, Viceroy of India and Chancellor of the Exchequer.

Frustration is one of the oldest of human complaints because it springs from our mortal nature. Like our shadow, it haunts us because we are body as well as mind and soul. Complete and satisfying fulfilment, when the broken arc gives way to the perfect round, belongs to another world than this. It is only as time is swallowed up in eternity that frustration shall be no more. Meanwhile the half light, the dubiety, the misunderstanding. We must accept a health that is vulnerable to illness, a knowledge that has its limitations, an experience that is not always one of clear shining. But ever and anon 'in the cleft of the rock' we are bidden to take note of those abiding certainties – the eternal might and mercy of God.

We can also apply this truth to what happens within us, that is, in our personal experience.

There are days when God seems withdrawn – and that for no apparent reason. We are not aware of any sin committed which should cause him to avert his face. 'More commonly,' Commissioner Francis Pearce used to say, 'I have to hold fast my confidence without a particle of conscious feeling to strengthen my faith.'

Again, this is not due so much to our sinfulness as to our humanity. Look, for example, at the index in Begbie's two volume life of the Founder and note how, next to the entries which refer to his energy, the largest number refers to those feelings of depression which clouded his spirit. When William James said that religious leaders have been distinguished by 'exalted emotional sensibility' varied by 'periodic melancholy', he could have set William Booth alongside George Fox whom he quoted.

We lesser mortals know those days when it seems as if the Lord said, 'My face shall not be seen.' Without reproaching ourselves with imaginary transgressions, we have to accept that clouded days are as much a part of the spiritual order as they are of the natural order.

This is true in the realm of thought. There are hours when the mind is fertile and hours when it is a complete blank. There are moments when ideas flow freely and moments when we labour with flint and steel without raising a spark.

So if spiritual dryness assails me, that is not – repeat not – specifically and solely due to the fact that I serve within a framework of Salvation Army discipline, but to the fact that I am a human being and not a robot. I have to accept the ebb as well as the flow as evidence of the reality of the tide. It is the Lord who gives and the same Lord who takes away. Both are divine activities and I have to learn to bless his name in both settings. I am not to bless lightly or irresponsibly for that would be almost as dreadful a blasphemy as to curse him. But I bless because, however dense and chilling the mists, experience will prove that he was close at hand even when I could not see him.

The supreme example of this is to be found in the Cross when Jesus cried out, 'My God, my God, why hast thou forsaken me?' However we understand that outcry, or whether we reverently conclude that here are depths we cannot plumb, it certainly looked to friend and foe alike that, wherever God was amid the darkness that covered the land from the sixth hour to the ninth, He was not with him who hung upon the Cross. Yet later, reflecting upon the finished work of Christ, the apostle saw that this was just where God was, never more truly with his beloved Son than in his act of atonement. 'God was in Christ, reconciling the world unto himself' (2 Corinthians 5:19).

And God will be with us in our hours of spiritual darkness. If his face be hidden, it is his own hand that hides it, for we have not to do with an absent God about whom we have gathered a limited amount of information, but with one who is livingly present and whose very refusals are at least a sign that he hears us when we pray. If he says 'no' to all we want, he will yet give us what we need, and 'in the cleft of the rock' will graciously reveal enough of his might and mercy for us to know that he lives and loves us still.

In this assurance I find sweetest rest!

Eleven

Lighten our Darkness

(given at an officers' meeting when the
Second World War was drawing to a close)

*2 Corinthians 4:8: 'We are troubled on every side,
yet not distressed; we are perplexed,
but not in despair;'*

ON 5 March 1945, Reinold von Thadden-
Trieglaff – subsequently founder of the Kirchentag
(or church day) in Germany – returned to his
country estate in Pomerania to find that Russian
troops, in their drive on Berlin, were already in
possession. Calling the villagers to the lakeside in the
morning for family prayers, he began to read aloud
the Scripture passage appointed for the day. 'We are
troubled on every side, yet not distressed; we are
perplexed, but not in despair; persecuted, but not
forsaken…'

Now it is against some such similar gloomy
backcloth that we must understand the apostle
saying that he was 'perplexed, but not in despair' (2
Corinthians 4:8). Those familiar with John Wesley's
Journal will recall his comment on the man who,
because his chimney smoked, complained to him:
'See what a cross I have to bear.' The apostle was not

making much ado about nothing – as is evident from his correspondence with believers in Corinth. There is more about his troubles in these two epistles than in any others he ever wrote. This could be because the Corinthians gave him most trouble.

He came to them (he said) 'weak, nervous and shaking with fear' (1 Corinthians 2:3 *NEB*). Of his experiences among them he wrote that he was 'pressed out of measure, above strength, insomuch that we despaired even of life' (2 Corinthians 1:8). Dare we say: almost gave up the ghost? Not far out when J. B. Phillips reads: 'We told ourselves that this was the end.' He'd had it! But this is all part of the realism of Scripture that would have us see men – even the greatest of them – as they really were. But this is also a realism that is unwilling to leave any man lying in the slough of despond. If the word is 'perplexed', it is also 'but not in despair'.

This apostolic testimony speaks to our condition – for who among us is not often perplexed – at times perplexed in our thinking; over our decision making; about our personal living. Take each in turn and begin with a simple illustration of the first.

1) In our *thinking*.

'I wish,' I once overheard an officer say, 'I understood what this "religionless Christianity" meant.' The phrase was continually being wrested to its own destruction. We cannot escape the climate in which we live, nor entirely avoid the phrases which bespatter the pages of our favourite religious weekly. I am the last one to say that an officer should be ignorant of current movements of thought, but no one should be led astray by what C. S. Lewis once called the chronological fallacy – that is, of supposing that the last phrase to be coined in a paperback or newspaper article is, for that reason, the one most surely to be believed.

Many of us would have been spared some confusion – and maybe one or two of our congregations even more – if we had understood that what Bonhoeffer meant by 'religion' was not what we usually mean. For us, religion is a loose synonym for Christianity. When we quote 'Pure religion and undefiled... is this...' we have nothing in mind but the Christian faith, the revelation of God in Christ. So to us 'religionless Christianity' sounds almost like a contradiction in terms, and we are correspondingly bewildered.

But Bonhoeffer set religion and revelation over against one another. Because of his theological upbringing (he had sat at the feet of Barth who entitled one chapter in his *Church Dogmatics* 'The revelation of God as the abolition of religion'), the word itself was weighed in the balances and found wanting. In his mind it stood for a religiosity that passed by on the other side.

From his cell he pleaded that those who professed Christ as Saviour should acknowledge him as Lord. This would result in a faith, working by love, that would seek to redeem the whole of life. But never did Bonhoeffer mean that any follower of Christ could neglect his Bible, or cease to pray, or neglect his Sunday worship.

Indeed, it was his regular Bible reading that, one day in June 1939, brought him to 2 Timothy 4:21 – 'Do thy diligence to come before winter.' This he took to be God's word for him as earlier Augustine had taken Romans 13:14, and on the strength of it he left the comparative safety of the United States for the martyrdom that eventually awaited him in Germany.

For my part I have no quarrel with new insights into the meaning of the word of God, nor with new ways of expressing old insights. However, the vogue of 'religionless Christianity', now dying away, is a warning of how a phrase can be mouthed without meaning. Not only with this phrase, but with all other theological catchwords, we should do as the climber does when reaching for a new handhold or foothold. He gives it a thorough testing before letting go his present grip and committing his weight wholly to the new one.

There is wisdom in the words: 'Test everything;' (1 Thessalonians 5:21 *Revised Standard Version*). This is not: reject everything. But prove all things. And in all your questionings never give way to the despair of unbelief. The Spirit of Truth is ours to lead us into all truth.

2) But equally we can be perplexed in our

decision making – particularly when our judgements affect the lives of our comrades.

In my apprentice days as a single captain I served under a divisional commander who had what we might would call a theme song. Ever and anon he would emerge into the general office where his principal colleague and I dwelt in peaceful co existence and begin to sing what was No 190 in the song book of my boyhood: 'The mistakes of my life have been many.'

The mistakes of my life! This had me puzzled – for I had been reared on the now obsolete dogma of the infallibility of Salvation Army leadership – at any rate from the level of divisional commanders upward.

But I have since learned what he meant. None of us is infallible, not even the youngest of us. And the more that hinges upon a decision, the greater our perplexity can be. I was therefore not altogether surprised, when reading the proofs of General Kitching's biography, *A Goodly Heritage*, to note his reply to Commissioner Norman Marshall when the former USA National Commander asked what would be his most satisfying experience on retirement. 'The freedom from the responsibility of making decisions affecting the well being of other people' was the reply.

The Apostle Paul knew something about this responsibility. He called it 'the care of all the churches'. For him this was no exercise in remote control, no academic directive issued from a permanent office. 'For three years, night and day,' he said, face to face with the Ephesian elders whom he had summoned to the island of Miletus, 'I never ceased to counsel each of you, and how I wept over you' (Acts 20:31 *NEB*).

We can enter into his feelings about his converts. There is no more sobering responsibility than to have a man's life in our hands – unless it be the lives of his children. So I can understand a fragment of a letter written in 1924 by General Bramwell Booth to Mrs Colonel X about her husband: 'Much as I wanted him for India I hesitated long before asking him to go because I thought of you and the children.'

How then can we make any final decision at all? Never self confidently, much less ever carelessly or casually. Off-the-cuff judgements, snap decisions, have no place in the affairs of the Kingdom. But we do have the assurance that the malice of men, as well as the mistakes of men, can be turned to the furtherance of the Kingdom. When that happens, therein can we rejoice.

'I have seen such a lot of mistakes overruled,' wrote Florence Allshorn. 'I used to think that other people had such power to dish your life but... I don't think so now. I believe that if you love God... you are fundamentally out of the hands of man.'

3) With more reason we are most often perplexed about ourselves (*personal living*), our own slow

growth in grace, our seemingly unending struggle with our own ingrained faults.

There is a bad and a good side to this sense of spiritual discouragement.

The bad side is that too much dwelling upon our imperfections can confirm us in those very faults we are seeking to eradicate. Indeed, such constant introspection can be a form of egoism. We are looking inwards instead of looking upwards. We are dwelling upon ourselves instead of looking unto Jesus who alone can deliver us from ourselves. There is great wisdom in forgetting the things which are behind, for only in so doing can we free ourselves to reach out for those things which are before.

It is agreed that some commentators relate this apostolic saying to the victories of the past. We are not to rest upon present laurels. But the word applies to past failures as well. There is no need to treat the past as a kind of hair shirt. I must not keep on reproaching myself for my blunders. If I must forget my victories I must forget my defeats also. If God has forgiven them then he has forgotten them. So don't let anyone keep on reminding God of what he has promised to remember no more. Treat yourself as generously as God is willing to do.

Of course, there is a good side to our perplexity over our spiritual shortcomings. Our refusal to be satisfied with ourselves as we are is a sign not of the absence of the Holy Spirit, but of his presence. To be spiritually discontented is a mark of grace, not a cause for further self despisings.

When *The Forsyte Saga* was being televised [in the 1960s] it reminded me that when the book first hit the headlines in the 20s, Donald Baillie remarked to a business friend that there must be a good many of Soames Forsyte's ilk working in the city. How did they feel about seeing themselves in the book? To which the answer was that even if they read the book they would not recognise their own portrait. They were too self satisfied to see themselves in the likeness of Soames Forsyte.

But we are dissatisfied. We are perplexed because at times it would be hard to recognise a picture of the Master in some of our thoughts and actions. That is all to the good. Perplexed we may be – but not unto despair – for while Jesus lives and grace is flowing we can yet become men and women after God's own heart. And this, not because we are sufficient in ourselves, but because our sufficiency is of God.

Twelve

A Lesson from History

(a centenary address in 1965)

*Isaiah 51:1-2: 'Look unto the rock whence ye
are hewn, and to the hole of the pit whence you
are digged. Look unto Abraham your father,
and unto Sarah that bare you: for I called
him alone, and blessed him, and increased him.'*

LIKE much of the latter part of the book of
Isaiah, these words were addressed to the Jews in
exile in Babylon, but they may be of help as we
address ourselves to the uncharted way of our
second century.

Of course, the exiles were very differently placed
from ourselves. They were in no mood for rejoicing.
'By the rivers of Babylon, there we sat down, yea, we
wept, when we remembered Zion' (Psalm 137:1).
And because there was so little in the present to
encourage hope for the future, the prophet bade his
countrymen remember their past. Not just the
golden age of David and Solomon. The contrast
between the glories of those days and their present
humiliation was too bitter to provide comfort. And
not even the more distant days of their deliverance
from Egypt, mighty act of God though that was.

Some of the exiles might well wonder how it was that a people who had once been set free from slavery were now slaves once more. But the prophet bade his countrymen look back to the creative act of God that had made them a people. 'Look unto Abraham your father.'

For their history as a people began with Abraham. That was where Stephen commenced when defending himself before the Sanhedrin. 'Men, brethren, and fathers, hearken; the God of glory appeared unto our father Abraham, when he was in Mesopotamia' (Acts 7:2). Let the exiles then look to the rock from whence they were hewn and the quarry from which they were dug.

As is clear from the first part of verse two, the rock was Abraham and the quarry (or pit) was Sarah. But as the second half of this verse makes equally clear, Israel owed her life as a people not to the human union of a man and his mate – Abraham and Sarah – but to the creative power of God.

'I called him alone,' means 'He was but one when I called him.' 'And I blessed him and made him many.' 'I' is the subject of that sentence and 'him' is the object. It was to God that Israel owed her commencement and her continuance. The cure for present despair was to look once again to Abraham. Spelled out more fully this meant: look at what God has done and then look at what man can – and should – do. Is not this what the Spirit is saying to us at this point in our own history?

Let Salvationists look to the rock whence they were hewn and the quarry from which they were dug. Our Abraham and Sarah are called William and Catherine. And look to them, not to suppose that we are merely of human origin but to mark how true it is to say: he was but one when I called him, but I blessed him and made him many. I gave him this unimagined increase – The Salvation Army.

To look to Abraham means first to look at what God did. For God's action preceded Abraham's response. Without God's call the patriarch would never have left his country and his kindred for a land he knew not of. Any wandering nomad of that day moved from well to well, from oasis to oasis, driven on by nothing more significant than physical need – the need of his flocks for water and of himself for food. What set this man apart from the desert tribesman of his day was that his movements were God guided and therefore God blessed.

So to look to Abraham is to be reminded of what alone gives significance and purpose to life. It was God's call in his heart and God's hand on his shoulder that made Abraham's life so meaningful. It was the outworking of God's purpose which blessed him and made him a blessing.

Yet there are those who almost fear the hand of God upon their life. They are near to dismay at the thought of what he may ask them to do or where he may tell them to go. But 'the land that I will show thee' may be no more remote than the nearby housing estate where there is no current Salvation Army activity. Or the young people's corps on a Sunday afternoon where a group of boys lack a company guard. Or the hall in the new town that we pass in order to soldier at the well attended hall in the old town. 'The land that I will show thee' may be nearer than we think. But the call to go and work there is as genuine a call from God as came to any character in Scripture – Old Testament and New Testament alike.

As with Abraham, God is calling us from the familiar to the unfamiliar; from the known and customary to the unknown and strange; from a settled routine to some new adventure, in his service. There is no knowing how God will use, or where he will send, the man upon whom he has laid his hand. But far from this truth provoking hesitancy or fear, it can be a source of supreme confidence. If God guides I can never be lost – not even if I am in a land I know not of. If all I do is as he directs, then there is no moment and no situation in which he cannot work for the furtherance of his redeeming purpose.

One holiday weekend many years ago one of our Australian bands was travelling by coach to a country engagement when a mechanical breakdown brought them to a halt near a bridge over a dried up creek. No band wants to be late for any fixture and, while repairs were being effected, the men did a spot of hymn tune practice. Then from under the bridge crawled a hobo, looking very much the worse for wear. He had been sleeping rough overnight and the music awoke him. It transpired that he had been a Salvationist – a bandmaster – himself, and it was not long before the drum became a mercy seat around which the men knelt to pray.

Is it not an exhilarating experience, one without parallel in any other field, to be working within an economy where even a mishap can be turned into a means of salvation? This is one way in which all things do work together for good for 'the called according to his purpose'.

To look to Abraham also means to look at what man can – and should – do.

'He went out not knowing whither he went' (Hebrews 11:8) is one New Testament comment on Abraham's answer to God's call. That is to say, his was a total obedience. His dedication was so complete that it included his own flesh and blood – witness the story of Isaac. Through his all-embracing consecration God was able to bless him and make him a blessing – as God has always done, and can do today, with any life that is unconditionally his.

It is sometimes said that if only we had this or that earlyday warrior with us again, what victories would not be ours once more. To such an observation I listen with respect for I yield place to none in my admiration for our fathers – and mothers – in the faith, the latchet of whose shoes we are not worthy to unloose. And yet is there not a measure of unreality in that desire? Those giants of the past cannot return. And we all have much more to do than to spend a single moment of our time crying for the moon.

I become uneasier still about this kind of talk if the inference is that without their return we cannot hope for a renewal of those blessings which were given in their day. Is it not the final impiety to assume that though God was mightily at work a century ago, he cannot so work today? This is really to limit the Holy One of Israel.

And I am still more ill at ease, almost to the point of doubting the sincerity of the speaker, if his expressed wish becomes his excuse for retiring to the sidelines. The present is nowhere near as good as the past, so I pray thee have me excused. So to reason – if reasoning is the correct description for such mental processes – is to dishonour those very greathearts whose memory is invoked.

What was it made our Abraham the greatest of them all? The completeness of his dedication. 'I early resolved that God should have all there was of William Booth.' And likewise our Sarah. 'I know not what he is about to do with me, but I have given myself entirely into his hands,' she said.

Their response, like that of Abraham, was unqualified. And we should no more waste our breath sighing for the return of the giants of the past unless with equal fervour we covet the Spirit by whose strength they subdued kingdoms, wrought righteousness and waxed valiant in fight. We cannot praise the total devotion of our fathers in the past and, at one and the same time, refuse to make a like dedication of ourselves in the present.

To sum up, God by his Spirit is saying to us through this ancient word: look at what I have done. And then, look at what you should do.

What he would have you do, do quickly.

Thirteen
Man's Continual Cry

Psalm 51:10: 'Create in me a clean heart,
O God; and renew a right spirit within me.'

TOWARD the end of Jack Lindsay's novel, *The Moment of Choice*, Kit Swinton returns from the funeral of his father to try to live again in mutual affection with his wife. 'Why have I been afraid to see the simple truth before?' he asks himself wearily. 'Why have I been ashamed of the desire to be good? Why did I have to go through this hell before I could bring myself to say to my wife: help me to live a decent life?'

The setting and language are 20th century. The word 'God' is nowhere used. But the remorse expressed by this town dweller is not far removed from that expressed in this penitential psalm which, according to the chapter heading in the *Authorized Version*, is attributed to David after he had planned the murder of Uriah in order to possess his wife. In fiction as in fact, life compels men to acknowledge the existence of those inner self contradictions which, apart from the grace of God, can be their ruin. Because of these character flaws, it is man's nature to be dissatisfied with his nature, but how to shape it nearer to his heart's desire is beyond him.

Now the Christian faith did not invent this dilemma. This is not a situation artificially contrived by the Church in order that men might feel their need for the ministrations of the Church. Both Jew and Greek – the joint fathers of our western culture – were aware of this all too human predicament and sought a remedy.

For example, the rabbis of our Lord's day taught that in man there were two natures, so that he was in the unhappy position of being drawn in opposite directions at one and the same time. He was – in the most literal sense – distracted; that is to say, he was drawn apart. And, though employing different terms, the Greeks said much the same. There has come down to our own times the familiar imagery of the soul as the charioteer whose unenviable task it was to drive in double harness two horses, one of noble breed, the other the exact opposite. The noble horse was reason; the untamed horse was passion – whose brute strength dragged the chariot earthwards.

To what the Greeks said the Romans added their own melancholy amen. When the Apostle Paul was in his early teens there died a Roman philosopher [Ovid], many of whose sayings can still be found in any standard dictionary of quotations. One such reads: 'I see and approve the better; I follow the worse.' And the apostle, who was a child of both worlds – Jewish and Gentile – summed up man's continuing plight in the well worn phrase: 'The good that I would I do not: but the evil which I would not, that I do. O wretched man that I am!' (Romans 7:19,24).

There is a sense in which we do not need to turn to Scripture for supporting evidence for man's unhappy condition. The Christian diagnosis of human need is not invalidated by a man's refusal to accept what the Bible says on this point though, of course, it is strongly supported if he does. But what is the truth to which our children are introduced when, in their study of English literature, they have as their set plays the tragedies of *Macbeth*, *Hamlet* or *King Lear*?

Now 'tragedy' was not the printer's word, nor the publisher's, but the playwright's. That was how Shakespeare himself thought of these fated men. And what was the essence of the tragedy save that, in each instance, a man of undoubted promise was ruined by some flaw in his own nature. Macbeth, for all his unquestioned physical courage, allowed ambition to become his master instead of his servant, and murdered both king and kinsman who stood in the way of the fulfilment of his dreams of greatness. Hamlet, of princely stock and of a thoughtful cast of mind, was the victim of his inner indecisiveness, the native hue of his resolution being 'sicklied o'er with the pale cast of thought... '. And

Lear's genuine affection, affronted by seeming gracelessness, exploded into wrath:

Ingratitude, thou marble hearted fiend,
More hideous, when thou show'st thee in a child,
Than the sea monster.

Nor are more modern instances lacking of this interior civil war – as when Dylan Thomas could say that 'I hold a beast, an angel and a madman in me, and my inquiry is as to their working and my problem is their subjugation'.

What has the Christian faith to say to this? First of all, it recognises that these are the facts of life. In the second place, it offers a remedy. That is to say, when the Christian faith speaks of men as sinners, it is not so much sitting in judgement on them as realistically accepting them for what they are. What is called the doctrine of original sin is this recognition of man's imperfections. Which is another way of saying that no social or material progress can – of its own outworking – eliminate that innate selfishness, which is the root of all sinful actions, from man's nature. Like his own shadow, man cannot be rid of this plague. Here is a literal old man of the sea whom he cannot shake off his shoulders. The Christian faith accepts these facts, and accepts them without despairing of their victim, because it can offer a remedy.

What is the remedy offered?

Three possibilities await man. The first is that there is no hope for him. As he is he will remain. The second is that man can mend his own ways. He can take himself in hand, lifting himself up, as it were, by his own hair. The third – which is the Christian possibility – is that man cannot change himself but that he can be changed or converted.

The first possibility is that there is no hope for man. You can't change human nature. But who says this? The apologist for current injustices, for one. Especially where the wrongs done to others work out, either directly or indirectly, to his own profit. It is in his interest so to let matters run. So he damps down all hopeful endeavour with his own self interested fatalism.

The drop-out echoes this attitude – because he himself doesn't want to be changed. He prefers to remain as he is. This is what Sally Trench found with some of the metho-dossers whom she tried to help. There were those who didn't want to be helped. Our Lord had to put a question of this kind to the cripple who had been lying at the pool of Bethesda for 38 years. 'Do you want to get better again?' (see John 5:6). For where there is no desire there can be little hope.

And the pessimist agrees that there is no hope for men, especially if he is a disillusioned intellectual. 'Man, who began in a cave behind a windbreak,' wrote H. G. Wells, 'will end in the disease-soaked ruins of a slum.' This should be seen for what it is – a counsel of despair.

The second possibility is that man can mend his own ways. He can lift himself up by his own bootstraps. Of course, it is open for anyone who desires to think this possible to do so. But on this the deserved comment is that there is not much evidence available to encourage such optimism, either for individuals or for society.

The truth is that if it be thought a vain dream to change human lives by means of the Christian faith, it is a vainer dream still to try to help men without it. It is always Jekyll who proves the undoing of Hyde. It is never our own unsupported desires for goodness which triumph over the evil which does so easily beset us. 'Iniquities prevail against me,' (Psalm 65:3) cried the psalmist. To the plea: 'Who on earth can set me free from the clutches of my own sinful nature?' there is but one answer: 'God alone, through Jesus Christ our Lord.'

This leaves the third possibility, the Christian one, that though man cannot change himself he can be changed.

Christian character is not and never can be self induced. No sleight of hand can produce Christlikeness from that doubtful mixture which we know unregenerate human nature to be. As well might the most skilful cook despair of producing a wholesome meal out of sour milk, rancid butter and stale flour. But despair of ourselves is not a bad thing if it leads us to cast ourselves without reserve upon the saving power of

God. The old proverb which declares that God helps those who help themselves is by no means the whole truth. The witness of the Christian gospel is that God waits to help the man who cannot help himself.

Hence the truth that 'the Lord's hand is not shortened, that it cannot save; neither his ear heavy, that it cannot hear' (Isaiah 59:1).

Fourteen

The Unity of the Spirit

(given at a united church service in South London
during a week of prayer for Christian unity)

*Romans 15:7: 'Receive ye one another,
as Christ also received us to the glory of God.'*

WITH these words the apostle comes to the personal appeal that concludes the main part of his inspired survey of the unifying power of the gospel. This survey is known to us as the epistle to the Romans, which gospel the apostle declares to be the power of God unto salvation.

First and foremost, the apostle sees this gospel as reconciling God and man. Man in his perversity had erected a barrier between God and himself which, on his side, he was powerless to remove. Yet where sin abounded grace had much more abounded. In the divine mercy a new and living way had been opened whereby man could come boldly to the Father's throne. The sons of ignorance and night could now cry 'Abba'. The long lost filial relationship could be restored.

Again, the apostle sees the gospel as uniting man with man – in the test case of the first century, Jew with Gentile. Between the two a great gulf had yawned. 'I will buy with you, sell with you, talk with you, walk with you, and so following; but I will not eat with you, drink with you, nor pray with you.' So Shylock. But the gospel had broken down this middle wall of partition. Paul's reasoning could be summarised: you were a Gentile; I was a Jew. God has made us both Christian.

And again, the same gospel united in a common fellowship believers of varying degrees of spiritual perception and judgement. The strong in the faith could enjoy fellowship with the weak. No differences of opinion need mar their unity in the Lord. Instead, they were to share and to bear one another's burdens. That is to say: believers of every hue were to accept each other in the Lord as he had accepted them. This do, and they would glorify God.

And how had Christ received them? We can answer that from our own experience for we know how he received us. To adapt Charlotte Elliott slightly:

Just as I am, thou didst *receive,*
Didst *welcome, pardon, cleanse, relieve.*

When we were no more worthy to be called his sons he ran to meet us with the kiss of forgiveness, transforming our woebegone appearance with robe and ring and shoes and, as a masterstroke, doing it all to music. Now, said the apostle, as freely and as generously as God for Christ's sake accepted you when, by everything in the rule book, you were not worth accepting, so accept one another. Spelling this out, this means that each of us – Presbyterian, Congregationalist, Methodist, Anglican, Friend, Roman Catholic, Orthodox, Baptist, Salvationist – is to be welcomed as he is for what he is. He is a man in Christ. The Spirit bids us welcome him as a brother beloved.

I must add that no one should applaud this New Testament directive too quickly or too lightly. In reality this is a hard saying – especially when translating this principle into practice. For us to accept one another as we now are rules out the possibility of any hard ecclesiastical bargaining. That is to say, to work for the kind of compromise born of the negotiating table that if you will abandon your claim to A I will forgo my right to B. For example, if all references to the Clarendon Code of 1661 are omitted from church histories published by the Saint Andrew Press, then the Society for Promoting Christian Knowledge would return the delicate compliment by eliminating from their publications any derogatory references to the National Covenant of 1638. More bluntly: if you will waive the use of incense I will disavow the tambourine. Both, by the way, were features of Old Testament worship.

But in the shape of things to come we are not seeking a kind of lowest common denominator of Christian faith and practice. In the interests of unity no church should be called upon to deny that movement of the Spirit of God which brought her into being, nor to repudiate those insights to which she felt – and, if she be a living church – still feels herself called upon to witness. A church of the future in which the Methodist participants had forgotten the hymns of Charles Wesley, or the Presbyterians the time honoured supremacy of the Word, or Salvationists their zeal for souls, would be a church from which the glory had departed. Our present divisions would be preferable – and, in my judgement, more serviceable – to God than such an emasculated body. The whole would be less than the sum of its parts – which would be intellectually absurd and spiritually calamitous.

For if we are to receive one another as Christ received us, then we must forget our imagined superiorities – our historical superiorities, for example, which can be a besetting temptation for the older communions; our fancied spiritual superiorities, a besetting temptation of the younger bodies, including my own. I may not say to anyone who calls Jesus Lord – and none can do so save by the Spirit – your worship is defective. And, by the same token, nor may anyone say to me – because you have not taken part in this particular ceremony you are none of his.

Unless it could be – and is this only a dream? – that in receiving one another we would remember not only how Christ received us, that is, as we were for what we were, but what he did in order so to receive us. For however we interpret those figures of speech by which we describe the relationship between the Father and the Son, it remains true that he who was rich for our sakes became poor. He who thought it not robbery to be equal with God made himself of no reputation and took upon himself the form of a servant and was made in the likeness of men. To repeat myself: he met us where we were as we were. He took on him the seed of Abraham, being made in all things like unto his brethren. J. B. Phillips summed it up in the word that 'He stripped himself of all privilege' (Philippians 2:7).

Does the hour find our churches great enough for that? To move toward one another as Christ moved toward us, as in divine generosity he accepted us as we were, sinful men whose only virtue was the grace of penitence? Penitence and acceptance; acceptance and penitence – are not these the root notes upon which any future harmonious relationships between Christian bodies alone can be based?

Before, like the rich young ruler, we turn away sorrowful – for the churches have great possessions, of historical prestige, of ecclesiastical status – ought we not to remember that in a small way we have already begun to act like this?

We have begun to act like this with our praise. I do not suppose your hymn books differ radically from my song book, but when I open to the pages on the Atonement, I find Isaac Watts next to Frederick Faber, who is next to Paulus Gerhardt, who is next to George Bennard. And when I turn to the nature of the gracious God, there stands John Henry Newman next to Joachim Neander next to James Montgomery next to Charles Wesley.

We have begun to act like this in our thinking – for when we turn to our bookshelves in the hope that they may lighten our intellectual darkness, we do not first regard an author's churchmanship. Thielicke and Trueblood and Temple stand side by side. All highly irregular, without doubt. But it is acceptance – and every new act of acceptance of the unqualified universality of the gospel is accompanied by a deepening sense of penitence for past blindness, whether intentional or unintentional.

We have begun to act like this with our witnessing. The many Christian fellowships in the city of London and elsewhere testify to a unity of spirit which transcends our ecclesiastical barriers. The same can be said of the Christian unions found in our comprehensive and grammar schools; of the House of Commons Christian Fellowship; of the unity of support – even though partial – given to the Billy Graham campaign at Earls Court.

In October 1965, 1 took part in an open air gathering held on a Saturday at noon in Union Square, San Francisco. This is perhaps one of the busiest parts of the city and this certainly one of the busiest hours. This religious meeting commenced with the local monsignor offering the invocation and concluded with the benediction pronounced by the president of the Californian State Baptist Association. I said my piece in the middle and was not conscious of bowing either to the right or to the left – though which was right and which left I leave you to say. But let there be no doubt – Jesus Christ was preached. And there were tambourines! And bands! And flags!

With much greater seriousness, when the call is to stand up and be counted in face of the foe, the thin red line may exhibit an untidy variety of uniforms but the spirit is one – as can be confirmed by reading either *Three Winters Cold, Captive in Korea* or *Valiant Dust*.

We have begun to act like this with our serving. Those who try to help the alcoholic (or the unwed mother or the social misfit) know that the first approach is not to ask his qualifications for being assisted – for he has none save his great need; but to accept him as he is, and this without a word of reproach or a trace of self righteousness, and yet, so delicate is the balance, without in the least condoning his misconduct.

As by grace the saints so receive the sinner, may they not by virtue of the same all-sufficient grace receive one another in unconditional fellowship in the Lord? Or are the signs that this is still too much to expect?

Fifteen

Borrowed from the Army Mother

(given at the Regent Hall to officers serving on
International Headquarters and associated headquarters)

FROM the Army Mother I borrow the title of a lecture, 'The Salvation Army and its relation to the Churches' that she delivered at the Cannon Street Hotel, London, on 20 March 1883. If we now follow where the saints have trod – it is only because this subject has to be rethought as generation succeeds to generation, and the current winds of ecumenism now require this of us.

It may help to begin with the conclusion, and then to indicate the stages by which this conclusion is reached. In brief: The Salvation Army owes it to its past, and equally to its present and future, to work in fellowship with the historic churches without loss of identity or of function.

In considering this matter certain facts of history, of geography and of theology have to be taken into account.

Of history – for it is sometimes forgotten that proposals for union (and the distinction between union and unity must never be overlooked) – were made by the Anglican Church to The Salvation

Army more than 80 years ago. Following discussion in convocation a committee was appointed, with the approval of the Archbishop of Canterbury, to approach William Booth on the possibility of the Army entering the fold of the church. The strength of the committee is an indication that the Anglican Church meant business, for its members included Dr Lightfoot (Bishop of Durham), Dr Benson (Bishop of Truro), Canon Wilkinson (later Bishop of Truro), Canon Westcott and Dr Randall Davidson (Dean of Windsor and chaplain to the Archbishop of Canterbury, later becoming the Primate himself).

One account of what happened can be read in chapter eight of General Bramwell Booth's *Echoes and Memories*, 'The Founder and the Bishops'. Some time later, in a much more casual way, there was an approach from Methodism, but nothing came of it. These facts are mentioned lest anyone should think that current talk of church union is wholly new so far as The Salvation Army is concerned.

Now much has been said in certain quarters about 'the sin of schism'. As when Alice and Humpty Dumpty were discussing the word 'glory', the phrase can mean whatever the speaker desires it shall mean. The use of the word 'sin' seems to presuppose the need for sorrow on account of sin, almost as if the uprising of certain religious movements in past centuries were actions now calling for penitence. Maybe; but on whose part?

It is true that even a limited knowledge of church history makes clear how mixed have been the motives which have influenced men. 'The Reformation' volume in the *Pelican History of the Church*, by Owen Chadwick, makes illuminating reading on this point. Pride and prejudice have played a larger part than is pleasant to admit. But while not denying this, it cannot be argued that a step taken in faith and obedience such as gave birth to The Salvation Army – or such as was taken by John Wesley in founding the societies of people called Methodists, or by George Fox in establishing the Society of Friends – is to be regarded now, or at any other time, as sinful.

To do so would be to call good evil and light darkness. To say this is not to think more highly of ourselves than we ought, but we cannot cast away our birthright. Had not the Army been raised up by God it would have perished long ago, for we had none but God on whom to rely. 'In those days,' wrote Catherine Booth, 'we had no funds or helpers except a few voluntary working men, the richest of whom were not earning more than 30 shillings [£1.50] a week.' Our survival is the Lord's doing.

Certain divine insights were given to William Booth which he felt he must obey. These have been transmitted to our care and to abandon them would be to commit spiritual suicide without cause. These could more properly be considered under the heading of theology but, to mention certain of them now, there is our standing conviction that there is no grace deemed to be mediated through the use of material elements which cannot be as fully received by faith alone.

Again, that in the ministry of grace there is neither male nor female. The gospel may be preached, the faithful shepherded, public worship conducted, a marriage solemnised and a saint laid to rest by a man or a woman, single or married, with equal acceptance in the sight of God.

Again, that salvation depends solely upon repentance and faith and that he whom God forgives needs no other absolution.

Again, that holiness has to do with persons not places, and is seen in Christlikeness of character.

Again, that certain patterns of daily living are required of those who acknowledge Jesus as Saviour and Lord, that my good can never be my neighbour's hurt, and that love is the fulfilling – not the abrogating – of the law.

Our history, brief though it is – for 100 years is as a watch in the night in the purposes of God – has made us witnesses to these truths. And I am not persuaded that any group of people is called upon to abandon those truths which God raised them up to declare unless and until God's people everywhere have accepted those truths. In that event the leaven will have done its work. The light from the candlestick will be shared by all that are in the house.

This is but one aspect of our church relationships for, as we witness before others, we learn from others. We are debtors to all men. The attitude which sees no good outside the Army is as deplorable as that which sees no good within. The song book which is in our hands every time we lead a meeting is but one illustration of what we – the youngest in the Father's house – owe to our elders. I believe in returning thanks. When we have done so, then we are better able to answer in a spirit of meekness those persons, lay and clerical, who so little understand us that – sometimes on our platforms as well as in private conversation they announce that the shape of things to come will mean our handing over of our spiritual ministry to 'the Church' while we retain our social services. This would indeed put asunder that which God has joined together.

Of geography – for an Army that is at work in all major continents has to consider the needs of all those continents. Dare it be said that in England the movement for reunion has been conceived in peculiarly English terms? Perhaps a Scot could venture such an observation. But suppose The Salvation Army was given terms on which we might enter the Anglican fold, to which fold should we join ourselves in France, or the Democratic Republic of Congo, or Chile, or Jamaica, or Japan, or Finland or the United States?

I put the question in all seriousness – is an

international fellowship that seeks to bring the universal gospel to all peoples and to unite all men everywhere as brothers for whom Christ died deliberately to destroy its own unity by joining specifically national limbs of the divine body?

Finally, and most importantly, of theology.

Here the clearest distinction must be made between unity and union. The World Council of Churches (WCC) itself has repeatedly disclaimed any thought that it is a piece of machinery for engineering administrative union between any of its member churches. The report on *The Church's Unity* issued by the Third Assembly in 1961 said: 'We are clear that unity does not imply simple uniformity of organisation, rite or expression.'

And again: 'Neither does this fellowship (i.e. that of God's people who make up the church universal) imply a rigid uniformity of structure, organisation or government. A lively variety marks corporate life in the one body of the one Spirit.'

The Executive Committee of the WCC which met in Odessa in February 1964, spelled this out afresh by referring to: '…the right of every church to hold its own particular attitude to the problem of church unity. [This] should be fully recognised and respected.'

Now it is a long standing rule with us to live, as far as in us lies, in unity and good fellowship with all other believers. In the lecture referred to at the commencement of this address, the Army Mother